Hook Into the ___

The Story of Mat Making
in North East England

Stories collected by Room For You Hospital Arts

ROOM
FOR YOU
hospital arts

Edited by Ellen Phethean

Tyne Bridge Publishing

Progging the Mat by Oliver Kilbourn, one of the Ashington Group of painters.

Contents

Heckle pin proggers, probably from Haggie's Rope Works, Wallsend.

Acknowledgements

Funding from the Heritage Lottery Fund and the Northern Rock Foundation made this project possible, but we couldn't have done it without the help of our fantastic volunteers.

We would also like to thank Beamish Museum, Newcastle Libraries, Northumberland Archives and Woodhorn Museum and the Ashington Group Trustees, Tyne & Wear Archives and Museums (Shipley), and Gateshead St Mary's Heritage Centre for all their support.

Most of all we sincerely thank all those who have so generously shared their stories with us, lent us their tools and their mats, and their time.

Silvie Fisch, Project Co-ordinator

Cover design: Jane Frazer

Illustrations ©Newcastle Libraries unless otherwise indicated.

Other photography by David Lawson and Ali Rhind.

Published in association with Room for You Hospital Arts by
City of Newcastle upon Tyne
Newcastle Libraries & Information Service
Tyne Bridge Publishing, 2011

www.tynebridgepublishing.co.uk
www.newcastle.gov.uk/libraries

ISBN: 978-1-85795-207-0

Two 'hi-tech' tools used for hooking from the back.

Printed by Elanders UK Ltd, North Tyneside

Over the years Ali Rhind and Rachel Phillimore have worked in all kinds of community settings with their hooks and proggers and, always, the wonderful family tales came pouring out. 'We had hoped one day to make a book that would celebrate the wealth of social history that is in the folk art of mat making. At last we have found a way to capture some of these evocative stories for you to share.'

Ali began working in community arts in the 1970s, with the Wallsend Hooky and Proggy Circle. She has been told many stories about mats, which she treasured but never wrote down – so the rich detail was lost.

However in 1998 she found herself a patient at the Northern Centre for Cancer Treatment, discussing with her friend Mary Jennings, who had also received treatment there, how hard the 'waiting' part of the treatment was. They talked about how the level of anxiety in the waiting room was often palpable. Mary's background was counselling, and the idea emerged that the combination of the two of them working together would be a good way to break the silence and get people talking to each other. They chose the activity that would bring the familiarity of every day past lives into the waiting room – a mat frame. Ali would be working on the frame in the waiting room, creating an easy focal point for starting a conversation for Mary, who would invite those waiting for treatment, as well as their friends and family, to join in. The resulting mats or wall hangings would be a great way to add some colour and warmth to the then rather gloomy waiting area. NCCT welcomed the idea and were lucky enough to get funding from the Northern Rock Foundation for a pilot project that eventually became **Room for You**.

Room for You started in 2001. Rachel became involved after a couple of years when they were able to extend their work from one

Ali Rhind, left, and Rachel Phillimore, with a wall hanging commissioned by Newcastle City Library in 2009.

day a week to three. Rachel had worked in community arts in rural Northumberland and Cumbria, where many patients come from with their own farming tales.

The core team has grown over the years, and today Ali and Rachel mostly work in the radiotherapy area with the mat frames. Many thousands of clippings have been put in by patients and their families. Some people have been inspired to go home and find the old mat frames in the attic or fashion a new pair to start making a rug.

Thoughts of the past and home are a comfort at a time when your world is completely challenged. The idea to start a memory book came from Ali. Artists and facilitators would be there with time to engage people in conversation, to encourage their stories and value them. At first they gathered the stories on sheets of paper, then later collected them into a book. It was covered with a distinctive patchwork fabric and over the years it has been handled lovingly, passed around the groups, laughed at, and recognised as a wonderful source of collective memories. The memory book became a focus for patients and carers alike, to remember and share past histories. Sometimes it was a bittersweet account of the tyranny of the matting frames – '*you can't go out to play until you have put a clippy in*'. But always it acknowledged the hardship and poverty, meaning '*We had very little, but the closeness we had then was a precious thing*'. These stories evoke familiar domestic memories: the smells and sounds of fireside scenes; the bread and baking; the order of the days of the week – wash day, ironing day, and baking day. The book captures the strong communities, the bonds of trust, the shared rituals and feelings that are easily lost with the passing of time.

The memory book is a lasting legacy of the **Room for You** project. The invitation to add a story to the book has been very important, as a recognition of the value of lives and the experiences that make individual histories. Some contributions in the memory book are anonymous, some contributors have since died: we wanted to acknowledge them all in this publication. People frequently tell stories about their lives through objects, and the family mat holds each family's history within it.

Rachel Phillimore and Ali Rhind

Chris Madge

The Memory Book.

6

Bodgy, broddy, clippy ...

Hooky, proggy, proddy, peggy, stobby, tabby ... are all names for those wonderful creations we know as rag mats, though in other parts of the country they are called rag rugs. You knew which part of the country you were in by the name given to the rag mat. They were made all over, mostly by working-class folk. The craft demonstrated recycling at its very best, making use of old clothes, stockings, blankets, flannel petticoats, uniforms and even what had once been the best suit. All could be cut into strips of material called clippings, ready to go into the mat.

Where and when did this rag rug technique originate? We cannot be sure of its exact origins, as little has been recorded from earliest times and later written accounts are largely conjecture. Sadly, therefore, not much is known of the early history of the craft; however it is thought to have originated in Europe, most likely Scandinavia, arriving in Britain sometime around the late 1400s.

It probably arrived in the North of England in late Tudor times. The Shetland Isles, (owned by Norway until the fifteenth century), may have provided a link between the countries' cultures. There was a strong tradition of rag rug making on the islands, which survived well into the twentieth century.

From Scotland, settlers took the craft to the eastern seaboard of America and Canada, where it reached new heights of artistic creation. In later years, ready printed patterns on hessian were exported from Canada and America to the British Isles.

Rag rugs were not heirlooms to be listed in inventories and diaries, and few written accounts mention them. It is known that the craft was never widely developed and was always regarded more as a thrift cottage industry, with the associated stigma of poverty. Although the making of rag rugs was an essential part of life in working-class homes in the rural and industrial areas of the North, it was also practised in other parts of the country, during the nineteenth and early twentieth centuries.

It was never considered respectable enough, however, to be included in the many needlework magazines of the Victorian period. Indeed very few examples of older mats survive, as, already being made from second and third hand material, when they eventually wore out, they were consigned to the dog kennel or rag and bone cart!

Often the whole family was involved in the making process; the menfolk constructed the large wooden frame and made the proggers and hooks; the women drew the designs and wove the clippings into the mat, while the children were given the job of cutting up the clothes to make clippings. Everyone did their bit and even the neighbours were roped in! Hardwearing, decorative, and above all useful, the mats helped to provide some warmth and took away the chill of the cold stone floors in many a farmhouse or pit cottage. Sometimes they were used as bed covers, especially when first completed.

Many accounts describe the excitement and furore of completing a new mat for a special occasion. A new mat in the parlour for Christmas or Easter was a 'must' for many families. Rag mats were made and used on every conceivable occasion, for the 'bottom drawer', for wedding presents and also at funerals. The long winter evenings provided an excellent opportunity for mat making, involving entire communities.

The austerities during the Second World War, when materials were in short supply, created a necessity to 'make do and mend', ushering in a new period of recycling. In the aftermath of the war, with the increased availability of wool thrums from the mills, together with cheap fitted carpets, rag mats went totally out of favour and survived only in museum collections, such as those at Beamish and Woodhorn.

By the 1960s, the gradual awareness that a wonderful craft was disappearing, led to a conscious revival by artist Winifred Nicholson working with some of the old Cumbrian mat makers, and the Barkers of Lanercost. The skill survived, imperceptibly changing from a craft to an art form. Louisa Creed, the niece of Winifred Nicholson, together with husband Lewis, took up the craft and Heather Ritchie from the Yorkshire Dales has taken it to Africa, fundraising to provide a livelihood for impoverished communities.

Many matting groups have been set up and the craft is now being enjoyed, not only as a communal pastime, helping to relieve the stress of modern living, but has also become invaluable in reminiscence and occupational therapy in residential homes and hospitals.

Using traditional techniques, artists such as Ali Rhind have transformed a traditional craft into a new language, based on contemporary materials and technologies. Today's discarded waste has become the art of the future, reflecting a current need for our way of life to become more 'green' and sustainable. Long may it continue!

Rosemary E. Allan
Retired Senior Keeper, Beamish Museum

Mam's Mat

When the summer months were over,
and the autumn frosts had come,
mam would look at our old fireside mat,
she'd say: 'It's going home.
I can't see that mat lasting
for much longer, I'll be bound,
we'll have to have a new one
before Santa Claus comes around.'

So starting that same evening,
she'd sort out our old clothes,
cut off all the buttons,
any lace or ribbon bows,
and, after that, would follow
many nights of busy snippings,
while the old clothes were converted
into piles of oblong clippings.
Then out she'd bring the prodders,
hessian sacks and frame,
and we'd all be looking forward to
the great mat making game.

The pattern would be trellis,
with dark border round as well,
and every little diamond
had a different tale to tell
in the clothes we'd worn
as we walked through life
backcloths of previous years:
a diary, worked in clippings
of our laughter and our tears.
And as mam worked, she talked about
the first few mats she'd made,
keeping house for her two brothers,
for their parents were both dead.

To help her make a mat
her chapel friends all came along,
and, as they sat there working
they would have a hymn singsong.
Then the next time that they came
her friends might bring along some others,
but mam said she knew that some girls
only came to see her brothers.

And as I watched her speak,
her eyes would grow a kind of haze
and she'd smile into the clippings
saying 'Oh my, those were the days.'
And in our conversations
I recall that mam once said
how some folks were so poor
they'd put their new mat on the bed.
I remember feeling thankful
that we weren't quite as poor
and when we'd finished our mat,
we could put it on the floor.

Then after weeks of working,
the great day finally came
when, to be hemmed and neatened,
it was taken from the frame.
And, in the winter evenings,
when we'd finished off our teas,
we'd keep warm round the fireside
on mam's mat of memories.

Edna Scott

The Heart of the House

In the days of large families, small houses and few resources, mats were made at the centre of the house, in the kitchen or living room by the hearth. The warm fire was the heart of family living and neighbourly visits: there would be a finished mat on the floor in front of the fire, while the new one was being made on a frame. So everyone lived their cramped lives around the mat making and as often as not, helped with it. The hooky and proggy activities in the hospital waiting room stirred many memories that illustrate the life and times of north eastern communities. Many remember much of the pleasure of mat-making in the old days was the social side of it – gathering together:

> I can picture my Gran's kitchen as clear as day: the big range, her proggy mats on the floor, a beaded shade on the gas light. The tin bath was kept on a hook outside and brought into the kitchen when my uncles came in from their shift … it didn't matter what else was going on, they had their bath regardless – they did wear something for modesty!

The fire was central to family living; it was often the only source of heat in the whole house:

> I can remember lying in front of the fire reading a book, and that must have been the most textured rug, every bit was tickling my legs. I can remember fighting the dogs, as the dogs liked being in front of the fire too. *Lisa Jenkinson*

> During the long winter nights we would sit beside a roaring coal fire and talk about the day's events, listen to the radio or recite our multiplication tables, while mam, armed with her favourite progger, would work away at clippy mats. *Memory Book*

> Our sitting room, 1948; Dad, Mam and I with the mat frames set up across two trestles and all of us busy. Dad worked at Reyrolle's engineering works in Hebburn, and he made me my own hook tool, which I still have, on the lathe. After an hour or so of absorbed working and talking, the frames were put in the large shed, which they shared with the chickens (almost everyone with a garden kept chickens as they had done during the war). We then got ready for supper, the coal fire glowing. My job was to toast thick slices of bread using a brass three-tine toasting fork. Mam was busy making tea and cocoa for me. I still prefer cocoa to drinking chocolate. Toast and butter with smoky scents is a delight and I miss it; electric toasters and grills do not give the same flavour and smells. *Brenda Rowe*

Beamish Museum

A kitchen range, with round oven and polished steel fender, in a typical miner's cottage from County Durham. A rag rug lies before the comforting fire and the little girl is probably sitting on a cracket or stool.

I was born at the end of the war, in Consett, which was a steel-making town high on a hill, very cold in the winter. The only memory I have really of mat making is my mother having the frame in front of the big black-leaded fireplace with the fire blazing up the chimney. *Vivienne Smith*

The fire needed to be burning all the time, with family members working round the clock on different shifts at the pits wanting baths and women cooking and baking every day. The rituals of the fireplace took on mythical proportions, the lighting of it, keeping it alight, and cleaning it out – all vital activities at the heart of family living:

> There was no such thing as central heating in them days, you had a nice fire in the living room with two ovens attached. My father used to try and set that fire so that the embers would burn almost until you got up the next

Working from the centre of the mat outwards, by the range.

> morning and it would keep the house warm to some degree. *Bill Scope*

The life-giving powers of the warm range were crucial for John:

> I was born early, at seven months through the pregnancy, and I spent my first two months in one of those ovens. They could control how hot it was so they kept me warm in there.

> We never had the luxury of fire in the bedrooms. That would have been soft ... when a fire was required in the sitting room my father never laid the fire. Our kitchen range was never out as it was needed for hot water, and Dad would stoke the kitchen fire until it was burning high and then thrust his shovel into the glowing heart and carry the flaming coals along the passage to the sitting room. I would have already been told to stand clear and would watch in awe as this godlike figure bore this volcanic shovel-full at arm's length to the waiting altar of the fireplace, trailing sparks and the smell of heat behind him. But, he never dropped the smallest piece of coal or burnt anything. I always regarded this as completely natural and was surprised later when people expressed horror at the idea. *Memory Book*

Whether taken from the 1930s or the 1960s, in rural Cumbria or pit villages in Durham or wider afield in Scotland or Nottingham, these stories of family and relationships, skills and work, poverty and making do, food and conversation and artistic imagination all start and end with the fireside, or the kitchen range.

The kitchen range

In those days of small flats and rented houses few people had a separate kitchen, dining room and sitting room; there was more likely to be a kitchen, scullery and front room, so the kitchen was where the family ate, lived, played and socialised. The range, with its ovens, hobs and boiler, took a lot of effort to keep clean, the stove would have been rubbed with 'Zebo' (black lead) then polished before it could be lit to boil water for a cup of tea. This had to be done every week. In front of the fire would be a clothes rack, and of course the rug. The rugs were a necessity because few families had carpets, there was often either a stone or wooden floor, and mats took 'the bareness off.'

Proggy mats were restricted to the scullery in our old flat. Scullery is a word that has very nearly disappeared from current usage. I suppose that the utility room is the modern equivalent, except that the scullery was so much more. We had a gas cooker in our scullery, which was used daily, but Mum always used the big kitchen range for bread making and cakes, feeling that the results were better. *Memory Book*

Quiet While the Bread Rises by Ashington Group painter James MacKenzie.

The social gathering

Mat making involved all the family from youngest to oldest. It included friends and neighbours too, and was often an opportunity for chatting, games and music. In the days before television, computers, iPods and electronic games, families were used to creating their own amusement.

> I think it was also an escape, they got a lot of comfort from being round the mat frame. Although it was necessity, it was a good excuse to go and have a chat and just relax. Because of the work ethic you were brought up with, you had to be busy. Even though they were sitting down, they were working. *Elsie Shaw*

It was mostly a winter time occupation – not many people recalled making them in the summer; and it helped while away the long dark nights for the family.

> I remember when I was young sitting around the coal fire on a cold winter's night with my mum, two brothers, three sisters and the baby in her pram. Mum would get out the old hessian potato sacks, then while my brothers were cutting up some of our old clothes and sheets, my sisters and I would be making them into proggy mats. *D.Gill from Blyth*

Because everyone made mats, when friends and neighbours called it was usual for them to take a turn with the mat making too. Family and friends would be chatting, having sweets and drinks, laughing, joking and singing as they worked around the coal fire. The large frames would often dominate the room and everyone had to weave their way through piles of clothes, some already cut in strips, others waiting to be cut.

For many people these were happy memories, a special time when children could be included with the adult company:

> The first thing I remember is the sore fingers (red raw) but I still wanted to carry on to try not to go to bed at the allotted time ... the family all being together, friends, neighbours, laughing, joking, singing. *Betty Ross*

Northumberland Archives

The Miles family of Ashington, 1932.

The children were used to listening to the adults and saying nothing, hoping no-one noticed them.

> Out came the prodders and we all had a turn … we always had one set of grandparents staying with us, so we were told of the things that happened in their past, as well as the things our own parents got up to – the very things we were always told we shouldn't do. So we all had a good laugh. Then one of the older ones would play the piano and we would have a great sing along, or maybe they put on the crystal radio and we would listen to music or even a play. *Mrs Glover*

Everyone had a task

Although some mat makers were very particular about their craft and wouldn't let anyone else do the hooking and progging, mat making was a time consuming activity. There were plenty of tasks that could be handed out to less skilled members of the family, particularly sorting and cutting. Often, the whole family joined in, even older brothers were encouraged to participate. The first job was to sort the used fabrics into colours and carefully trim them down into narrow strips. The strips would be rolled into balls and placed in a basket until required. When the mat maker ran out of a particular colour he or she would commandeer one of the family to make more.

The task of cutting the clippings was given to children more often than not. The women would teach the younger ones to cut scraps of rag, wool, any material, into strips roughly six inches long by about one and a half inches wide. A visit to a grandmother would usually involve evenings and sometimes days, especially when the weather was bad, helping in, or hindering the making of the clippy mats. Some tasks were preferred to others:

> There were little bits of arguments about who did the cutting and who did the progging and who did the cleaning … the cutting was the hardest bit … the best job was progging and the best job of all was finally cleaning the finished mat, clipping all the tops off to make it level. *Bill Scope*

> If you were very very, very lucky you got to use the progger and put some bits in yourself. *Helen Webster*

On the other hand, children could be quite a nuisance at times:

> 'Meg Miller's pullin' a mat in the morn!' Up goes the battle cry in the 'pit rows' at Throckley. This was the signal for the neighbours to hunt out their 'hookers' and 'proggers'; they wouldn't have to hunt far though as they were more or less in constant use. The lasses would gather with their tools and their kids – us, then the fun would start; there seemed to be a pecking order on the mat frame. Some would be engaged cutting

clippings. Us kids would be in the den under the mat chewing the cinder toffee that was always part of the job and just kept coming. Many a 'lug' was 'clipped' at this stage for 'pullin' the clippies oot!' 'Come oot i there ya little b...s or ahl morder ye's!' – I can still hear Big Meg's voice. *R. Hogg*

It took my Gran quite a while to finish these mats as, unknown to her, I would sit under the mats, out of sight, pulling the pieces out quite quickly until I was found out and checked quite strongly, in other words smacked. *Joan Hepple*

As there was no heating in the rest of the house, it was inevitable that people gravitated to the warmth of the fire and were drawn in to the craft of mat making. As the mat grew, so did the friendships.

Imagine the early 1960s – a young, rather shy but handsome Asian student from Nairobi arrived in Sunderland to do a degree in Pharmacy. He was introduced to the art of hooky and proggy textiles, and spent many long winter evenings by the fire with his landlady making clippie mats – one way to keep warm! This young man eventually met a student from the Teachers' Training College and in 1967 they married. Thirty-seven years later we have one beautiful daughter and super son-in-law. *Heather Thakkar*

Some of my happiest memories as a young girl were spent in my Grandmother's company at Embleton, in her rambling farmhouse at Wynyard. The household consisted of Grandad, Granny, the unmarried members of the family – Uncle Willie (known as Boy – such was the importance in those days of producing a son and heir), Uncle Fred, Uncle George and Auntie Bella. Then there were five servant men and three servant girls. Of course every loaf of bread was baked in the kitchen oven on the old black range; every morsel of food for all those hungry mouths was home cooked, and every item of clothing possible was made by hand ...

... Upstairs in that

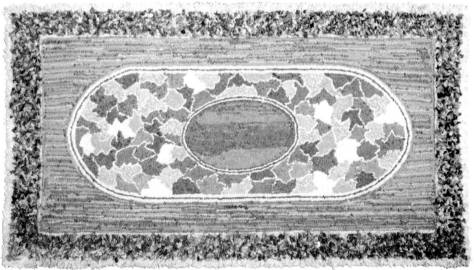

Beamish Museum

This unusual combination of hooky and proggy mat was made by Miss Eva Milner at Priory Farm, Castleside, in the 1940s.

16

lovely rambling stone house in one of the smallest (and chilliest) bedrooms was the Quilting Room. Here my Grandmother, together with the other female members of the household, spent most afternoon hours (except Sunday, when it was forbidden to touch a needle) working on hand-sewn quilts for the beds. At milking time of course the young women had to go to their various chores in the cow byre ...

... Our feet were kept warm in the Quilting Room in individual boxes of hay, freshly gathered once a week from the stack in the yard. I still have one of Granny's quilts, as warm and as pretty as ever! The aim was always to have the new hearth mat to put down for Christmas; so we (including servants) sat working 'on the mat' in the dim light of the oil lamps. *Margaret Kingston*

When the new mats came off the frame they often went in front of the fire – the king position.

And it was gorgeous to put your feet on. *A. O'Brien from Rosehill*

I know the war was on and things were bad, but the house to me was warm, a big fire and lots of love! *Brenda Porter*

Milkmaids, Northumberland, around 1900.

The Craft

Although there are various terms for the craft: hooky, proggy, proddy, peggy, stobby, clippy, cleeky, bodgy, tabby, tab and clooty, the process was more or less the same across the country and hasn't changed with time.

The frame

'Geordie, when you've got a spare minute, tighten these trestles up for me will tha?' Alan from Esh, a mining village in County Durham, remembers his Gran saying. She was talking about the frame. The mat making began with a frame made of lengths of wood; two long bars with slots in each end and two thin flat ends or stretchers that fitted through the slots in the rails. Hessian would be stretched tightly across the frame as a basis for the hooky work. Men would make the frames, often using skills and materials from their trades – the shipyards, the collieries or retail work. So the colliery joiner might make the frame, or provide the wherewithal.

> My father worked on the old coal-fired ferryboats that went between North Shields and South Shields. There used to be so much stuff floating about in the Tyne then, and he'd got some pieces of hardwood out of the river to make into a mat frame. When it was made he polished it. He was the one who made the proggy mats. *Memory Book*

Otherwise, the frames were improvised from whatever was to hand; all sorts would be pressed into service to make what was needed.

> Dad made the frames from an old door frame. He put the poker into the fire to make it red hot, and put the holes in with the red hot poker. *Ray Ditchburn*

Old beds were a common source of frames. Margaret Brooks remembers, at the end of the Second

World War, the air raid shelter that had been built between their yard and that of the flat upstairs was demolished and the bunk beds that had been in the air raid shelter were broken up. Her father salvaged the wood to make a mat frame.

One woman explained the frame she worked on was much bigger than the one being used at the hospital by Ali and Rachel and it was on a pivot so you could turn it over to see the work you had done. It could be worked on at both ends.

The frame resting on trestles or chairs.

If there wasn't wood handy to make frames, the household furniture was adapted: one woman said her mother turned the big kitchen table upside down and tied the four corners of the sugar sack to the legs to keep the mat stretched while she was working on it. A great big frame might be propped between two tables, or stretched over two or three chairs.

Eileen Foullis recalls setting up the frame with peg holes different spaces apart so the frame could be adapted to the size of mat to be made – 'It stretched the hessian taut so you could put the clippings in.'

Otterburn, 1890s.

Work on the new mat would begin in about August or September, and the frame would become part of everyday living for the months running up to Christmas. The frames might be kept in a cupboard under the stairs and they'd be pulled out at night, 'well they took quite a bit of room up you know, but you thought nothing of it.'

Or they would become a permanent feature while the mat was on the go:

> A large canvas pinned to a wooden frame was always in the kitchen. We all ducked under and slid around it, but didn't mind at all as we could incorporate it in all sorts of childhood games on rainy days.

One story from the Memory Book recalled how a set of frames was painted with bright images, decorated in a similar way to a narrow boat.

Sewing the second side of the hessian to the binding.

The hessian sacking

The hessian was sewn on to webbing, which was attached to the wooden frame. The hessian, also called the harn, or canvas, could be bought by the yard at the local co-op or draper's. Not everyone could afford to buy brand new hessian for mats, and at times during the war it was scarce, so people were inventive about acquiring supplies.

A. Vickerby said his dad would get the hessian from the horse keeper at the colliery; it started life as the sacks of hay for the pit ponies:

> We called these sacks 'choppy bags', these were split in half and made a good size mat for in front of the fire.

Canvas doors were used in the roadways of the pit to stop the wind where the tub rails went along. These were appropriated when new, before they had been hung, and being a yard wide, were ideal for the mats. *Lucy Milton (research for Tyne & Wear Museums)*

In the local Co-op, customers would ask for empty sacks of any kind. Coal, sugar and, best of all, coffee, were much sought after. They could be unpicked and washed, and used when hessian was not readily available.

In the rural areas, the backing was usually sacking that had held farm stuff and the sacks were washed and fitted together to make whatever size was wanted. The sacking would be hemmed, to give extra strength to the edge of the mat. Its weave was coarse enough to allow the pieces of material to penetrate it, but close enough for them to be held in place. *Lucy Milton*

The next step in the process would be to stretch it across the frame and stitch it to the fabric already hammered around the edge.

F. Bell explained how his mother would get a candle and run the strong thread across it to wax it – that was for stitching the sacking onto the frame. The size of the hessian determined the size of mat; the size of mat would also determine where it would finally end up in the house, and also dictate what kind of pattern and colour scheme would be suitable.

When the mats were finished they were taken out of the frames and the hessian ends were sewn down to give them a neat edge.

TWAM, Shipley Art Gallery

Assembling the frame.

The Tools

A variety of tools were needed, depending on the style of mat. These tools were rarely bought ready-made, so using the skills of family members or begging favours from fellow workers and neighbours, they were lovingly crafted and then guarded carefully until the mat making season began.

Some remembered steel tools with turned boxwood handles or tools made entirely of metal:

My Grandad used to make steel proggers at the Close Works foundry – for whoever needed them. He made a claw hammer himself and it's still in the family – my youngest daughter has it. *N. Purdy*

My father was a 'trimmer' on the colliery boats, and he sometimes made mat frames and tools too. *Memory Book*

Pointed tools were prodders or proggers, used for clippy mats.

Our proggers were quite long, 4-5 inches, wooden and polished. This was in Yorkshire where I was growing up. *Memory Book*

Trevor Read said his mother had two, six inches long, and he imagined:

Me Dad would'a had them made at the pit by somebody, probably the blacksmith. They were metal with a big knob at one end, a fat bit in the middle and then a point. No hook. We used them in later years to keep the rabbit hutches closed.

Not everyone had custom-made tools. Anything could be improvised. Many recalled the prodders were made out of shaved down dolly pegs:

Well, mine was an old peg – you would snap the legs off and then sharpen it down to a point. I've got some that were made out of ships' rivets filed down. You used anything that had a point because you couldn't go out and buy tools. *Margaret Atkinson*

In the dales, where sheepfarming was prevalent, a boy might adapt a bit of sheep's horn to make a prodder, then polish it and engrave his sweetheart's initials into it as a gift for her.

Different proggers made from a variety of natural materials:
Top, a pair of wooden whittled proggers.
Middle, a prodder made from a dolly peg.
Bottom, sheep and deer horn proggers from a rural farming community.

Mrs Graham started making mats in the winter of 1947 when the snow was so deep no one could go anywhere; she was pregnant and she and her mother-in-law sat either side of the frame. Later in her pregnancy the doctor told her she shouldn't be sitting matting all day, but should get out for some exercise.

> We used to peel an apple or an orange and use the swirly skin to draw the border shape; the outside border was always black. Our material came from a factory in Yorkshire and there were lovely colours.

Mrs Graham's World War Two progger made from the windscreen of a crashed plane.

In the Second World War, a plane crashed above Wark, and Mrs Graham's husband walked up onto the fell and retrieved a part of the windscreen, from this he made her a progger. She described him having to melt it to make the right shape. She made mats for many years and proudly sent one to America to her grandson.

The other type of tool had hooks and/or holes. This was for the hooky-type mat, where one long continuous strip of material was hooked through the hessian, giving a the finished mat a different appearance.

This progger has been crafted from an old organ stop.

These tools were described as either small with a hook on the end or a little larger with two holes through which the longer pieces of material were fed.

A hook that has been made from an old file.

Two hooks made in the pit forge from an old bolt and a nail.

Another really important tool was scissors. They were needed to cut the material to the correct size and to trim the finished rug. Sheep shears were sometimes used for this task, and all the tools would be kept carefully alongside the frames, waiting for use.

People would search for a shape that would sit comfortably in their hand, and then would hang on to their specially made tools.

We all had our own favourite proggers and woe betide anyone using someone else's! *Sheila Jeffrey*

Wooden gauges for cutting clippings.

A brass hook and steel progger.

Nineteenth-Century Canadian Rug Rhyme

I am the family wardrobe, best and worst
Of all generations, from the first;
Grandpa's Sunday-go-to-meetin' coat,
And the woollen muffler he wore at his throat;
Grandma's shawl, that came from Fayal;
Ma's wedding gown, three times turned and once let down,
Which once was plum but now turned brown;
Pat's red flannels, that made him itch;
Pants and shirts; petticoat and skirts;
From one or another, but I can't tell which.
Tread carefully, because you see, if you scuff me,
You scratch the bark of the family tree.

A hooky mat.

25

The clippings

Every scrap of material was saved, often for months, before enough was accumulated to make a mat. Old woollen blankets, suits, coats, linings (long johns) and tweed were taken apart and washed. The material was cut into strips about ⅜ inch wide and these were variously named cloots, or clippings. Long strips were for hooky mats, short strips for clippy. Some people recommended that the cloots should be about the length of a matchbox, saying that if they were any longer you would have to clip the mat, that meant going over it with scissors, to ensure the clippings were even length. Some cut shorter, about an inch long while others preferred very long clippings of up to four inches. These would be stored in bags or baskets, waiting for use. For the hooky mats, materials were washed and cut into long strips, then wound up into a ball.

> When I was little my Nana asked me to cut a lot of clothes up. I thought she was barmy. But she made the strips of clothes into a beautiful rug of a sunset scene. It was a lot of different shades of oranges and yellows and reds. I loved that rug. *Memory Book*

Some clippings were made at home, others could be purchased; a variety of sources were scoured for just the right colour and texture, but they were all made from recycled materials. Jumble sales were a regular source of clothes for ripping, tearing, cutting up:

> Mam made all her clippings from old coats, skirts, jumpers, wool blankets and anything else that was suitable, even dying the blankets to get the colours best suited to particular designs. All the clippings were stored in large cardboard boxes and she would have neat piles of assorted colours in front of her as she worked. *Memory Book*

In those days ladies' lisle stockings were thick, so they were used.

> Nothing got wasted, my dad's army uniform, and his demob suit went into a clippie mat. *Memory Book*

Old blankets were useful and could be dyed.

> When I came to set up our home we didn't know what to do for the stairs. I saw these army blankets in a second-hand shop – a grey colour. So I thought I could dye them in the gas boiler and I dyed them a rust colour for the stair carpet. *Elspeth Wilson*

> We used to use onion skins to get brown, and flowers to dye the material. *Margaret Atkinson*

Bought dyes were easily available and the old wash house boilers and tin baths came in handy.

Hunting for old clothes at the Quayside Market, Newcastle, 1899.
Clothes would be worn and worn, only the very oldest could be used for clippings.

There used to be a shop at the top of the road called Cummings. Miss Cummings sold everything from a screw to dyes; you name it, she had it, hammers, anything. Father used to send us with coppers for a dye and a tin. He had a huge tin bath and four buckets. You had to cut pieces of material, anything from a skirt to an old pair of trousers to size. If they were a light colour Father had a red dye, a green dye, a yellow one and a blue. First he had to make his dyes in these four buckets and he put them on top of the cooker. He couldn't make a mess – I can see my mother's face, a very fussy woman. He used to stir it with a wooden paddle, just a piece of wood that he'd shaped and sanded, and we would help. When it reached a certain temperature, they would be brought out into the back yard where my sister and I couldn't touch them, then he filled the tin bath and he'd put them in to steep. Me mam used to make him go right down to the bottom of the garden. I can see it yet, because she was very, very just so, he was the same. You never saw him, even when he was in his work clothes, untidy without a shirt and tie, you never saw him looking dirty. *Brenda Noble*

There were a number of suppliers of ready-made clippings, too. Some women made a business out of collecting clippings so they could sell them. Workplace scraps were another valuable source.

In 1863, the North of England Co-operative Society was founded. By 1872, it had become known as the Co-operative Wholesale Society (CWS). They had a big manufactory in South Tyneside:

Beamish Museum

> My mother and father and my sister all worked at the CWS factory at Pelaw – they were able to get lots of leftovers from the bedcovers and eiderdowns being made. They would roll the pieces up and bring them home. *Memory Book*

Commercial stores knew the value of the scraps. One large store's carpet department sold clippings at 1s 11d per pound. The clippings were purchased from salesmen who visited the store regularly, they were delivered in large bales, which were then sorted into bins according to colour. The clippings were waste material from clothing manufacturers. Some factories sold them by the stone. Five-shilling bundles of blanket ends could also be purchased from mills. Baize, bought from clothing shops or the Co-op, was used to outline and fill in patterns. This was thick wool stuff, not thin felt, and came in a variety of bright colours but, even so, some complained it did not wear well. In rural areas and smaller towns, bespoke tailors would sell a sack of small pieces of cloth for one shilling. These were prized as they were brand new tweeds and suitings of good quality, and of course the tailor was glad to get rid of them. *Lucy Milton*

We talk about saving the world now, but I think they were saving the world then because they couldn't afford to throw things out – it wasn't a throw away society then, they just used what they could. I suppose you had a bag and you just put all the stuff in and then you had a great day sorting it all out, and hopefully you had enough. *Mavis Jopling*

Lisa Jenkinson remembered a rug:

> It was heavy, incredible heavy, really heavy, far heavier than you expected, I was quite small at the time as I can remember feeling almost crushed by the weight of this rug.

This was because of the tightly packed material, but, as Eileen Foullis recalled,

> You tried to put the clippings in tight so not to create gaps where you would see the hessian (so the tighter you progged the hessian the better).

Some people had definite preferences:

> Oh I liked the proggy better than the hooky ... it's quicker, the hooky, but I liked the proggy 'cos it's more fluffy. When they were new they were quite luxurious really. They were lovely ... like stepping on a thick carpet.
> *Memory Book*

Despite the hard work, some savoured the hours spent making a mat, saying the experience was soothing, restful and a change from everyday work, with something nice and useful at the end of it – a sort of achievement. Many women and men found it an outlet for their creativity.

This family group were proud enough to stand on a home-made mat for this posed portrait, around 1920.

Community Spirit

In the nineteenth and until the late twentieth centuries, communities were more stable. People lived where the work was, and often as not their house was provided by their employer, whether the railway, mines or shipyards. Families were large and often the entire family might be engaged in the same or similar work, as Lillian Johnson remembers:

> I'm one of thirteen and I'm the last one that's left. My father and several brothers were all miners. Two brothers were joiners, one was a blacksmith at another pit and the other one worked in a factory.

Employment, or lack of it, was a shared experience for a family, neighbourhood, village or town. Even those not directly employed in the major industry might work in related jobs, thus schools, shops, transport would all be affected by its fortunes, and this tied the community together. As families expanded, children grew up and began their own families. They often remained in the area, maintaining a close-knit society going back generations, like Brenda Noble's:

> Growing up in this crescent, 74 years from a child, I went to school at West Moor, so did my sister and my son went to school there also, and to be quite honest I knew nothing else but Firtree.

Neighbours knew each other, adult women were known as 'aunties', and they all looked out for the children in the street:

Children in Newcastle, around 1938.

In those days, neighbours were friendly, not like they are today. I mean, we knew everybody around here and if we were doing anything we shouldn't, they never lifted their hands but their tongues were enough. Everyone knew each other's business and troubles, as all were in the same boat. *Brenda Noble*

I loved my childhood in that mining village. Although I was an only child and my parents both came from small families I had myriad 'aunts', 'uncles' and 'cousins', all of whom were really neighbours but in the close-knit community that you always found in the colliery villages there was more than a bloodline that bound you together: tragedies, celebrations, a hard-working life and a local chapel. Dad worked in the mines all of his life, apart from the years he spent in the army during the Second World War. He survived an explosion at the pit he worked at and Granda was killed by a fall of stone at the pit during the war. Every family was scarred by working in the mines and each family was frightened when they saw the navy blue NCB ambulance appear in the street. Was it their turn for some misfortune? *Elizabeth Gardiner*

North Shields.

Despite, or perhaps because of, hard times, the community relied on, and trusted, each other:

Somebody in the family usually, or on my side of the family anyway, could play piano or a mouth organ or something. It wasn't unusual, maybe once a week, just to have a bit of a get-together and a singsong. And you couldn't afford anything other than tea, but it was the community, the camaraderie, which I suppose to a degree you got in these little mining villages where everybody knew everybody else. The Cambois I knew is not there any more. The colliery rows: Boathouse Terrace, Bridge Street, Chapel Row, Sea View, have all gone. And if you had a parcel to deliver – you might have a parcel for number 37 and if they'd gone across to Blyth for some reason and had maybe locked their door. Somebody, maybe at number 10 would say 'fetch it down here.' From 37 to 10 – so it's not just next door, it's the other end of the street sort of thing. And it wasn't uncommon, and also as I said, a lot of people just didn't bother locking their doors. 'Ah, just stick it in there postie. They've gone down to Blyth, they'll not be long.' I mean you go down to Blyth, by the time they've walked down to the ferry, done the crossing, done their shopping they'll be away about three hours at least. *Michael Wilkinson*

Because everyone needed mats, and everyone made them, it's not surprising the whole family would join together to help each other with the task.

1947 was a hard winter, a long period of deep lying snow added to the gloom of post-war Britain, with rationing still very much on people's minds. Gathered around the kitchen fire-grate, 'Geordie' folks burnt anything that would add to the warmth of the gas-lit kitchen. As a child, I remember the women passed the long dark nights gathered around the kitchen table, with the object of producing the 'clippie mat,' a pastime, which I am sure lives in the memories of elderly people to this day. *Bob Hunter*

We lived in Carville Road, Wallsend and my Aunt May lived upstairs. She was a great pastry cook and always had a hooky mat on the go. She would knock three times on the floor with a brush: this was the sign for Mam and me to go upstairs. It was my job to cut the material into strips or short pieces. We all sat around the frame talking while we worked. At the end of the night we would all have home-made meat and potato pie with mushy peas. *Jean Boston*

Children knew the importance of making the mat, it was a much needed item as well as a sociable night in, and they learnt family stories, and understood adult concerns. In those communal days, children were closer to adults' work and they had to show respect for it – like not playing in certain streets, if the men were on night shift. *Memory Book*

It would not occur to children to refuse to help:

I can never, ever remember my mam saying to me that I HAD to do anything. But when she said 'would you like to' there was absolutely no doubt you had to. Sometimes there were things you really, really wouldn't like to do but still you did them with a smile on your face. Where now I think if you said to children – would you like to go out in the rain, down to the shops and carry potatoes? They would probably say no. There was eight of us and you just all had to help, whether it was making bread or emptying the upstairs potty, because there was an outside toilet, to going out in the rain or cleaning the nappies. I still sometimes make bread with the children you know. But it's not a case of necessity now. We do it now to show them that not everything's got to be factory made. Them days it was done through necessity. *Elizabeth Wilkinson*

Ancrum Street, Spital Tongues, 1920s.

Mrs S. Bell / Newcastle Libraries

Ouse Street, Newcastle, around 1935.

Mat clubs and the WI

All kinds of clubs were common in the pre Welfare State days, often combining a mixture of social, educational and welfare services, such as The Miner's Welfare, Working Men's Clubs, The Workers' Educational Association (the WEA was founded in 1903 in order to support the educational needs of working men and women), through to leek clubs and allotment societies.

My father was in a cycling club and my mother once told me the members of the club gave them a clippy rug as a wedding present in 1927. It had a dark background and a yellow wheel in the centre. Just imagine that on a wedding present list today – and why not! *Lila Anderson*

The St James Cycling Club, Newcastle, 1930s.

Many areas set up their own 'mat clubs', sometimes forming co-operatives to pool resources and skills. A group of women would pay so much a week and their names would be drawn from a hat. The group would work on a mat together, and as each mat was finished the one whose name was drawn would get the mat.

In the school holidays in the early fifties (I would be about seven or eight years old) I loved clippy or clooty mat day. My mother had the frames and stretchers for making the mats, and once or twice a week these would be set up and mam and three friends (all neighbours and my 'aunties') would sit around the mat all working together on the design. There would be four mats to be worked and everyone put their name in a hat and first name out got the completed mat, and subsequent names the second, third and fourth mat. *Memory Book*

Alternatively, a woman would work on her own for the club; the members would save their clippings and give them to the club, in other cases their weekly payment would provide the material, and pay the mat maker for her time and effort. These clubs were common in mining areas where widows or wives of miners were struggling on the bread line, especially through the 1920s. The mat work for the individual maker would bring in extra income to feed the family.

There were other institutions that helped draw people together, such as the church or the Women's Institute. Edna Newman had vague memories of one WI branch in Northumberland trying to teach the skills of mat making to rural children. What she did remember vividly was their organisation of trips and events, rare for the likes of Edna, a young girl in service seventy years ago:

I went to live at Warkworth and the nearest Institute was Shilbottle. The chauffeur's wife, the gardener's wife, the parlour maid and the housemaid were all members. The chauffeur happened to have his car and he took us right up to Shilbottle. Membership was half-a-crown, and for sixpence you got your supper, and a penny raffle. It was October and the Christmas party was going to be in December, in a wooden hall across

Beamish Museum

This family group gathered around a mat-making frame was photographed in the Derwentside area during the 1892 Miners' Strike.

the field from the old schools. Oh I thought, well I want to go to that party but a half-a-crown was a lot of money in them days. So never mind, I paid me half crown to become a member. When we came out it was black dark. And I can always remember the Coquet Island light was flashing as we walked down that road and I'd always think it was a leading light. *Edna Newman*

Families together

Often all the family members would be roped in to share the work, especially the unpicking and cutting up of old clothes, which was a long and tedious process, before the mat could be started.

Jim Winter from Pity Me explained how the jobs were given out to help his mother:

> My sister sorted the colours, I cut or tore the clippings. My elder brothers took turns at the frames, while mother was preparing food.

> I remember sitting under the mat being worked (it was like my tent!) and being rewarded with cakes, scones etc., which had been baked by the 'aunties' for their 'mat' day and washed down with tea or my treat, pop. *Irene Pearson*

The radio would be on, for music or favourite programmes:

> When my sister and me were helping with making a mat at home, the wireless used to be on. We were so convinced that someone was inside the wireless doing the talking that we made a hole in the fabric part to peer in … Well we were just children. *Memory Book*

It was expected that a visit to grandparents would involve helping with the mat. It kept children out of mischief and speeded up the making process.

> It was one of my tasks to cut the bands of material so she could get the mats done for example, for Christmas, to put down in front of the fireplace. I was eager to try doing the mats but I had to wait until I had mastered the art of cutting the strips of material to the right width (I found out later it was to keep me busy as she only had one proggy tool). *E. Cox*

However, hidden under the mat, children could get up to all sorts of things:

> When I was four I used to sit in a clothes basket with clippings in, which was under the mat frame. I had a lovely fringe. One day, when I sat in the basket, I found the scissors and cut my fringe off, straight across. My mum played war with us afterwards and I had to get out of the basket. *Memory Book*

> In 1946 my young brother Alan had measles and was in bed. Our kind mother set up a mat frame and started making a hooky mat in Alan's bedroom to keep him company. However, other duties called and the mat and child were left alone. Thereupon Alan set to and pulled out the strips of wool so carefully put in to the mat. As he was regarded as ill, he got away with his naughtiness. I think the mat was completed when Alan was better. *Sheila Jones*

Mats were made at all times of the year, but it was most important to have a new mat for Christmas. There was often a race to get it finished and down on the floor for visiting relatives and neighbours to admire.

> Over seventy years ago, two of my lovely unmarried aunts lived with my Grandma and my three cousins, Joan, Carol and Ann. There were also foster girls in the house, as many as three at any time. So when we went to see them, my dad and my brother were in a house of eleven females. I loved it, lots of fun and laughter, though I was amazed at the looped sanitary towel hung round the bedroom door to stop it banging! I don't know what dad and Peter thought. I thought they were the best family in the world. My cousins thought we brought the pleasure with us. It wasn't

November 1934, a family group around the Christmas tree. Mother seems to be playing Santa Claus.

Beamish Museum

till many years later I discovered a whole truth: we made the joy together.

Money was short and everybody helped to make proggy mats. The most spectacular one was in place when we arrived for Christmas one year. I can vividly remember the wonderful colours of the stair carpet. Yes! It was a long, awesome carpet all the way from downstairs round the landing to the top. The odd thing is, we must have had a stair carpet, in our house and I have no memory of it. My auntie's stair carpet was a very smart colourful patchwork separated with black cuttings made from hundreds of fabrics. It was an outstanding achievement that was admired by every visitor.

More surprises that Christmas when mam tried to play carols at the piano. There was a terrible noise instead of 'Angels'. Grandma had hidden the presents behind the front panel of the piano and they were pressing on the keys. *Sheila Boyle*

Finishing off the mats. These ladies were photographed at Rookhope, Weardale, in the 1920s.

A very fine hooky mat, so fine it is hard to believe it came from rags. The mat was made at Steel, Hexham.

When a mat was on the frames, children would spend hours cutting the materials to help out. This was the least favourite job and most time-consuming before the more exciting part of developing the picture could begin. Some of the material they used was extremely tough, and many people referred to the weight of the scissors. They weren't as sharp as modern day scissors, people would have grooves in their fingers and aching hands by the time they had finished cutting.

Reluctant family members had to be enticed to do their share. Children would have to do a bit of the mat before they could go out to play, or a parent would offer sixpence to go to the pictures if a young person did a bit of the mat first.

Me mother used to make mats. We had a big set of frames, and everybody used to have to muck in. And as we got older, when we went to school, when we came home at night, all them that came from school, had to do a ball. Me mother used to roll up balls of cut old clothes and everybody used to get a ball and what we call a progger ... you had to put that ball into the mat before you got your tea, usually a bit of jam and bread or a bit of bread and dripping, but never very much. I can remember that quite well. *George Patterson, Beamish Oral History Collection*

We used to sit under the frame of the mat and cut the clippings from old coats and skirts. We had hours of fun and a bag of sweets from our war rations to share with our friends. We didn't run the roads like they do today; our mothers knew where we were – even when we were 21! *Mary Gibson*

On mat making night Grandfather made lots of toffee, for treats, only if you did your share of cutting up an overcoat made of fustian which was very, very thick. The coat bowed you down, the weight was so heavy. Cutting this material also cut into your fingers, it hurt. *Memory Book*

She put a quarter of peanuts in the middle of the mat frame and to my delight the peanuts would jump up and down as they put the clippings in. When the mat was finished the frame would go to the next person's house and the 'clippy night' would be at their house until the next mat was finished – and so it would go on. *Sheelagh Ward*

All the neighbours helped each other too.

There were two particular families on the street that we were very friendly with. Sometimes we would be in their house making a mat or they would be in our house making a mat. If they came to visit you when a mat was on the go they just got a prog and worked on the mat as well. *Bill Scope*

'Slip up to Auntie Meggie's and ask her for the loan of the mat frames'. That was my mother, it was 1937 and I was ten years old. We lived in the east end of North Shields and Auntie Meggie lived on the Balkwell estate over a mile away. I had recently acquired a much prized bicycle so off I pedalled. Auntie Meggie said 'I gave them to your Auntie Nellie three weeks ago but I'm sure that she will have finished her mat by now.' It was only a short distance to my other aunt's house and Auntie Meggie was right – the

Peggy's toffee

½ lb marg or butter
1 lb golden syrup
1 lb sugar
1 large tin of condensed milk
vanilla essence

Melt sugar and marg – stir until melted (not quite boiling), add warmed syrup – stir until well mixed – pour condensed milk in – stir for 25 mins, then test by dropping into cold water until hard. (It can take a bit longer) Add vanilla stir and pour into greased tin, score for breaking later.
Peggy says half an hour progging deserves a bit of toffee'!

Peggy Webber's toffee recipe was a favourite at Wallsend Hooky and Proggy Circle in the 1970s.

frames were available. 'Oh, and don't forget to take the bag of bits' said Auntie Nellie. A short length of old clothes line enabled me to sling the frame pieces over my shoulder and with the bag of bits (which was quite large) straddling the crossbar of my bicycle, the required equipment was home in no time and set up for production. *Memory Book*

In those pre-war days there were, of course, no plastic charity bags regularly appearing on the doorsteps. Discarded clothing was sorted, the woollens going to 'Baty's' yielding fourpence per pound weight. Other suitable materials went into the 'bag of bits' and the remainder into the dustbin. There was consequently a good supply of materials available for

Children playing shops with 'boody', pretty stones or pieces of glass found in the street, Newcastle, around 1900.

hooky or clippy mats. Co-operation existed among family, friends and neighbours to maintain the supply and of course there was much unofficial competition to determine who could complete the most colourful and complex designs.

In days of hand-me-downs, clothes were passed on as a child grew. An item might be worn by many siblings, so it's not surprising they held strong associations for the whole family. As they sat round the mat frame, Grandmother would tell stories of where each piece of material came from. The memories were literally woven into the mat: carefully kept baby clothes, Dad's first day at school, a special evening dress or a favourite coat. Then the owner could sit reminiscing: 'Eeh, I loved that coat' or 'By, mind that had good use, we all wore it at some time.' 'Ee that were our Nellie's coat there – she wore nothing else for years.'

In fact it could become a way of remembering a lost relative: one woman had kept lots of her mother's clothes after she died. One day she sorted all of them out, and cut them into thin strips. She worked very hard and made a huge rug out of them; she still had it thirteen years later.

However, not every story was so touching – Peggy Webber made a commemorative golden wedding anniversary rug with portraits of herself and her husband. She confided to Ali Rhind that when she got cross with her husband, she would go and jump all over his face to vent her frustration (see page 97).

And not everyone was so enthusiastic about a house full of matters:

One day I came home to find the living room filled with ladies all sitting around a wooden frame over which was stretched hessian, with a pile of coloured strips of cloth of many colours by each of them: they were making a 'clippie mat'. A joint and jolly social event. For me though, it just seemed like my home had been taken over, with all the snug and secure atmosphere gone, as it was on wash days when damp clothes hung everywhere. *Alan Bays*

Evelyn Barton's sister went missing:

I remember years ago when my younger sister was about eight years old she went missing while playing out in the street. Mam searched all over and was getting quite concerned for her. Then she remembered seeing Eileen, my sister, playing with the girl next door who was part of a family of thirteen. Mam knocked next door and asked if their daughter had seen Eileen. The neighbour, Mrs Pawd, said all her children were in bed but she asked Mam to come in and she would speak to her daughters. She led Mam into the bedroom and said to her, 'You see all of my children are in bed,' and she began to count them lying top to bottom in the bed. 'One, two, three, four, five, six, seven, eight.' Then again, 'One, two, three, four, five, six, seven, eight, nine. That's funny,' she said, 'There should only be eight.' Then out popped Eileen from the middle of everyone, smiling. Guess what was on the bed for blankets? Yes, proggy and clippy mats to keep them all warm. So they weren't always used for the floors.

This memory highlights the trust and closeness between neighbours and their intertwined lives.

Life was much simpler then but I believe much happier. *Memory Book*

Sandgate, Newcastle, around 1898.

We loved our pretend theatre and we would stage our 'plays' in the backyard using the clothes horse as a dressing room. Our 'theatre curtains' were someone's old blankets from the bed slung over clothes line. Our parents' old clothes and bits of net curtains were used for costumes, we loved to dress up and we had really good imaginations. The clothes horse with a blanket over it also doubled as a tent, what a versatile object this was. There was hardly any rehearsing and no script but we loved to entertain in our make-believe world. We would perform to anyone who would watch. *Elizabeth Gardiner*

Being a bus conductor, Newcastle, around 1938.

Games and imaginative play entertained the children of the past century in a way that many people, rightly or wrongly, feel has disappeared:

Sadly these times will never return because the mines have gone and the communities have broken up. I am sad about the break up of the communities but not so sad about the mines going. I personally don't think anybody should be asked to work in the bowels of the earth. The cost of the coal was the cost of lives, lives like that of my granda and many others who died for a pittance and, in those days, no compensation and very little thanks. Many other families were affected by 'the pit disease' pneumoconiosis and other bronchial diseases such as emphysema and chronic bronchitis. Some still suffer today approximately twenty years after most deep mines were closed. *Elizabeth Gardiner*

Despite the bitter legacy of the heavy industries, Elizabeth felt 'very proud of my ancestry and my family's mining history.' It is clear that hooky and proggy mats are a proud symbol of that history and community spirit for many people.

It is a long, long time since I saw a clippie mat in its pride of place, in front of the fire, but I'm sure I am just one of thousands and thousands of the elderly, who remember its place, in the households of working class people. *Bob Hunter*

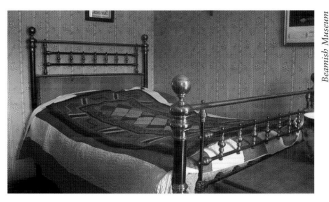

Clooty Rugs by Reta McBeath c1936

We bide at Forty Millar Street, in
Carnoustie, by the sea,
An if ye care to come in-by,
It's welcome ye will be.
Jist noo we're afu' busy, rippin' up
breeks an' coats,
For wir Faither's makin' fireside rugs,
oot o' orra cloots.

Ye've really nae idea, what a nacky
job it is,
Tae get the greens, an' reds an' blues,
A tae harmonise.
In the corner by the winda', wir
Mither rives an' tugs,
Tae supply the raw material, for
Wir Faither's clooty rugs.

First he tacks a sugar pock
firm on tae the frame,
An syne he draws a pattern on't
tae keep it neat an' trim.
Noo tae start the border, says he-
'Dae ye think we'll hae enough.
For ye ken, tae work a border,
Ye need a lot o' stuff'.

Noo he's got the border finished, there's
the diamond tae be dune.
Says Paw tae Maw, 'I'm getting on,
I'll finish this ane syne.
Noo tear up some o' that, it'll mak
a bonny centre,
This'll be a cosy rug, by the
fireside in the winter.'

Bellingham Carers' Group making a mat.

44

Patterns and Pictures

The different processes created different styles of mat: the clippy, with the loose ends on the right side, was like a very big pile carpet, while the hooked method created a smooth, rounded effect. So the pattern varied according to which style of mat was being made, where in the house the mat was going to be put down, and how large it was. If it was a bedside runner that had less wear, it might be made of paler pastel colours, or if a fireside hearth mat was planned, it would be darker, perhaps with bright spots of colour, to absorb the everyday dirt and wear it would receive. However, like magic, a piece of dull hessian was soon transformed, taking on a life of its own.

> The long winter evenings were spent 'on the mat.' New mats were made each year with all and sundry joining in. There were 'cutters' cutting up the clips into their various shapes depending on whether we were making a 'clippy', a 'runny' or a 'proddy.' These always had a dark border made from outworn socks or dark clothing. Various patterns were dictated by the amount of clips. Nothing in the household was wasted and the mat was made on sacking from the farm. Our pleasures were simple but very satisfying; we were all very happy in those far off days. Alas, the farm is in total disrepair now – those happy days are gone never to return. *Margaret Kingston*

The pattern

Patterns had to be drawn on to the hessian, or sometimes they were transferred from a paper pattern or a wooden template that some enterprising artist had made: 'Dad made all his own patterns using wooden templates he made himself from a kind of plywood.' Later on, hessian mats with designs stamped on them were available. These could be bought at the Co-op and other factory outlets, though they were more expensive to buy and many considered

TWAM, Shipley Art Gallery

the hessian was of inferior quality, although they saved time and work because they came ready hemmed.

Drawing patterns was seen as a skilled job; it usually fell to one member of the family or neighbourhood, who had been recognised as having an artistic eye, as Yvonne Bruggy from the St Mary's Matters' Group explained:

> I should imagine it was my grandfather who did the designs because he was quite artistic (during the war when we couldn't get wall paper he stencilled little flowers all over the entire room to make it look as if it was wallpapered) ... they were fairly simple designs – with a dark edge and just whatever fabric came to hand.

Because mat making was a communal activity, however, agreeing a pattern could take some time and one or two arguments before everyone was satisfied. With little money for buying ready-made patterns, most people would make their own designs using books, dinner plates, egg cups, bottles and other kitchen utensils. This was the usual way to develop a pattern, which would consist largely of round lines and circles, or straight lines and squares, and the most popular shape – a diamond. They were sometimes drawn freehand, and sometimes they were marked out in flower patterns to make a change from the monotony of lines. They would be drawn in chalk, ink, crayons or indelible pencils with wetted points. In the thirties, the Sunray design was very popular. Dennis and Evelyn Lee, who worked in Annfield Plain Co-op, described it as:

> Rays of the sun coming up from the corner. So this end was sort of Sunray, semi-circular, and then it was graded down in colours. *Beamish Oral History.*

A corner template.

Drawing the patterns.

Mat makers often copied ready-made patterns, or other rugs they saw, which led to similarities in design, as Ali remembers.

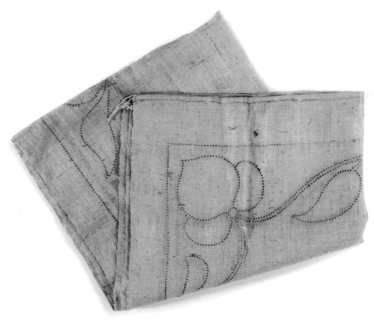

> Back in the late 1970s we visited every house in a street somewhere near Charlotte Street, Wallsend, to canvas their ideas about a mural that was planned for the end of the terrace. In that one street, sixteen houses still had a mat on the floor, but what was even stranger was that nearly every one was a version of the same design, whether smaller, larger, hooked or proggy, dark or cheerful. When I asked, they told me that everyone would go along to the man at No. 43 to borrow his 'good wooden template' to draw around. *Ali Rhind*

A pre-printed pattern by Barlow's.

People had their own designs and they were handed down and added to from generation to generation. Bill Scope explained how he learned to help his father put the patterns in.

> There were some lovely patterns, in fact the fireside rugs you see today were very reminiscent of the patterns that you used at that time. Me father would either have a circle in the centre or a diamond and other times he would put rough squiggles across the mat.

If there wasn't enough material to make a particular pattern in set colours, then a more abstract approach was necessary. Bill Scope said he preferred making these clippy mats, because:

> What I used to like making was the miscellaneous patterns. You used to get all the colours, and mix them up in a bag so you had them all at random. You couldn't see what the plan was, because you were working on the back of the mat. When you had a plan, you knew what it was going to be like when you turned it over. When you made the miscellaneous ones, you could stick some bright reds, bright yellows, bright greens, any bright colour you could get your hands on, all over the place. When it was finished you turned it over and cleaned it. It was just a conglomeration of colour – just like looking at a rainbow sometimes, because the colours were that good.

Because it was a communal enterprise, the end result would often reflect the many hands that had helped to make the mat:

> The funniest part of it was when a mat was on the floor, you could tell exactly how many had been at that mat. Everybody was different. She once took a half-done mat, it was wool. The woman paid a lot of money for the wool and when that mat was finished it was a lovely but you could tell exactly where she started, you see some put them in slacker than others. You could tell straight away on the pattern, but it didn't matter because the pile used to be flattened down with walking on it. *Mrs Rutter, Beamish Oral History Collection*

Colours and designs

Often, though, there were few colours available, which limited the possibilities. The usual pattern wasn't a complicated style. Whether there was a special pattern or not, most mats had a border – the majority consisted of a dark border, with a repeating shape for each corner, often a diamond, sometimes an inner border, then any bright material was used for the centre.

> Well, me mother always had a border first and that was either grey or black, and me father used to put whatever she wanted on it. Sometimes she had a moon – half moon in each corner with a star in the middle, with the star a different colour, and the middle was mixed. *Lillian Johnson*

Proggy designs were usually relatively simple as the rough surface didn't show complicated patterns well. Hooky mats could be more intricate as patterns stood out clearly on the surface.

> I did not like proggy mats. I had a childish fear of them. Terry Pratchett wrote a child's book called 'The Carpet Dwellers' and that encapsulates my feelings perfectly. I always walked around our mat if I could, as I was nervous that something might jump out and bite me. I must stress that my mother was very house proud and that our proggy mat was regularly taken into the back lane, thrown over a line and vigorously beaten. She probably beat them out of existence and that is why they were continually being replaced. Clippy mats were entirely different. I liked them and did have a go at making them. As I remember, the designs were usually rather severe or geometric, squares bisecting circles and jagged dark stripes streaming across a lighter background. I liked the designs, which I think, looking back through mists of memory, were probably diluted Art Deco. But I could not stand the colours which I described as mud and sand; a range of beiges and dark browns with the occasional splash of a bilious green or orange. They were, however, better than the proggies because they were not so dark and dismal. These clippie mats were never very big, probably because of the cost of the wool. When the clippies were finished my father had an enormous pair of scissors, which he used to cut the pile as level and as close as possible. They usually made half crescents

that went in front of the fireplaces in the living and sitting rooms. *Memory Book*

The need for dark colours on the kitchen mats that had pit boots walking across them regularly, or for particular colours in a pattern meant the whole family had to be roped in to gather and hoard the right material.

> The first thing I remember is having to save up everything navy blue for about a year (maybe it was shorter; it was during the war). The special mat I remember was a hooky. The navy blue was the background, with red tulips for the design. The whole mat was oval and there was a thin white border. I remember my mam tucking the hessian behind and sewing it to get the shape. *Sheila Spour*

> When we went on a holiday to Wales we sometimes picked blueberries to get a deep blue dye.

> I seem to remember a lot o' them were blue – dark blues and light blues – so blue must've been a colour that you could get easily. *Memory Book*

Everyone saved up their old clothes and bits and pieces to help, and it was exciting when patterned or bright coloured clothing like tartan and Fair Isle jumpers were added to the mix.

> My Granny had a family of sisters with big families who collected all their old clothes for her. These were mostly in browns, greys, black and especially navy blue. Granny loved to come across a bit of bright material to work into the pattern with the broken gipsy-peg shaped on the edge of the doorstep. She was the dab hand at pegging so she made her sisters' hearth rugs as well. Her patterns were mostly diamonds and triangles but all different from each other. *Memory Book*

Alison McGowan remembers a particular rug made by her dad when he was at sea in the Merchant Navy – It was two shades of green – bottle green and a lighter green. 'The pattern was in squares and stripes which I used to imagine were furrows in a green field.'

A move up in the world, to Billy Row near Crook in County Durham, and having a house with stairs for the first time meant:

> My mam made a stair carpet in loopy – she put a border up the sides, then mixed colours for the rest.
> *Memory Book*

Formal designs were often taken from traditional motifs such as key, thistle or scroll. Some were taken from quilting patterns such as the Prince of Wales Feathers, which were very popular.

Flowers brought bright touches of scarcer colour. Some mats had a pattern of red roses in the corners and the middle.

> My uncles were miners and they made so many things, among them were clippy mats and lovely patterns:
> Peony Rose. They really were very beautiful. *Memory Book*

Rugs often featured animals that would have surrounded the communities in earlier times, such as a horse with a foal:

Beamish Museum

A proggy mat celebrating Queen Victoria's Diamond Jubilee, 1887.

This very 'bullish' bull from Cumbria was designed by the Barkers of Lanercost.

Going back about sixty years, my brother being sixteen years old, worked in the shipyards. He had an accident, broke his leg so was off work. Wanting something to do, he made a mat frame and, it being summer, went and sat in the backyard where he lived and he made a hooky mat. He drew a rabbit on the hessian and worked it in from one end of the mat to the other. When it was laid down on the floor and you came in the living room door, the first thing that greeted you was the rabbit. It had pride of place. *Memory Book*

One big mat had a picture of a Pekinese dog and then some of the places the owner used to take it for a walk – such as the Spanish City in Whitley Bay, which Bob Corner remembered: 'My mother used to ride on her bike with that dog in the basket in front.'

A woman who'd worked on a farm near Chatton in her youth was fond of a black farm horse. Some years later she asked her husband to draw out the black mare on the sacking and she made a mat in its memory. A skilled mat maker could make a work of art:

My favourite was the big tiger, absolutely beautiful. It was laid in front of the fire and really was eye-catching. Then in each bedroom she'd made a mat with crinoline ladies, beside the beds. Her mats were outstanding. *Memory Book*

My last clippy mat my Gran made was of a house-garden and one big black cat called Sammy. My Gran used to chalk her pattern on the sacking then my Grandad would tack the sacking onto the frame, then lift the frame onto a large wooden table. As soon as that was done our cat would lie in the middle. My Gran chalked around him. My Grandad cut some shiny black material for us to fill the outlines of Sammy. My Granny sewed two glass buttons on for his eyes and a little pink one for his nose.

This hooky mat is being cut off the frame. It has a wide border from a template and the middle is a crazy paving design which was a very common choice.

My uncle took the mat to Germany but he died there so we don't know what happened to it. But it was fun helping to make it. *Isabelle Curtis*

Great pride was taken in an ambitious design, and there was often rivalry between families to do the most colourful and complex patterns:

> Way back in the forties and early fifties, when I was just a kid, my Grandad Purdy and Grandma used to make hooky mats and proggy mats. My Grandad worked as a pit deputy and was very good at art and mat making, and put his art into his mats. New mats had to be made for Christmas ... three were castles, Alnwick Castle for the fireside rug, Bothal Castle for the door mat and Warkworth Castle for the runner. And once there was a mat set with butterflies on and one set made with cottage and garden, then one small door mat, with Santa and sack and a snowman with a little boy waiting for his gift from Santa. You know, that was one of the times I looked forward to and nearly all pitmen's houses had this type of mat, it was one to beat the other. *Memory Book*

Whatever the political outlook, socialist or royalist, some rugs were too prized and precious for the kitchen floor:

Chopwell had a close association with the coal miners in Moscow, Russia, who funded the miners of Chopwell during the long miners' strike. Since that period Chopwell was always referred to locally as Little Moscow. One of the miners' wives made a large clippy mat, of a large hammer and sickle, the Russian flag emblem, drawn on the hessian by her husband. When she had completed it, she laid it on the floor ready for him returning home from work. When he arrived home, he took one look at it and said, 'That's too good to wipe your feet on.' He took it up and hung it on the wall, where it remained until he died. *Memory Book*

Harry Bolton, leader of the Chopwell miners and a councillor, addresses a meeting in the 1920s. The Chopwell Lodge DMA banner, with its portraits of Keir Hardie, Marx and Lenin, forms a backdrop.

One day the Queen Mother came to visit South Shields. One family, who lived across from South Shields Town Hall, owned a rug in the colours and style of a Union Jack:

> So my grandmother got the rug up off the floor and draped it out over the window for everyone to see as the Queen Mother drove past. *Memory Book*

Some patterns depicted characters and scenes such as a Dutch boy and girl, a windmill, and a sailing ship.

> Whenever we reminisce about the old colliery villages, coal fires and mat making, my husband repeats his favourite proggy mat story. He went rushing home from school one day, sat down at the mat his mother was making and progged the initials 'J. H.' into it. 'What is all that about?' said his mother. 'A new girl started at our school today and her name is Joyce Harle' he answered. He was then seven years old and I was six, and my family had just moved to the village. We became playmates, then sweethearts and have been happily married for fifty-six years. *Joyce Morgan*

Sadly, since Joyce recorded this memory, her husband has died.

Elizabeth Blair remembers a very extraordinary pattern:

> My friend Doreen told me a family story which still makes me smile to this day. It happened before she had even started school. The family had been working on a large mat together. The children of the family were looking forward to seeing it on the floor in front of their large open coal-fire. It was an exciting time. (Children liked to try and identify and show everybody the bits that had been their clothes.) With due ceremony the mat was laid. She remembered her older brother saying he was going to be the first to walk on it. As he did so he pretended to trip up and their mother told them to stop being silly. He told Doreen he'd fallen over the cap that was on the mat and said she should pick it up in case somebody else tripped. She remembered going to try and pick it up, which amused her big brother no end. It was the definite shape of a man's cap. It appeared, like magic, in the randomly mixed centre of the mat. Her mother was quite upset, she recalled, but soon saw the funny side of it. It was a source of great laughter in her home for many years. People who visited always acted as though there was a real cap there. Some would cross the mat and 'step' over it. Others would make a slight detour round it. Children tried to pick it up. Even the family who knew it wasn't real got caught out. The children in the family thought it was hilarious.

Ali Rhind

Clara Vale villagers made a commemorative mat to celebrate their Village Centenary in 1991. The mat was hung opposite the Clara Vale Pit banner in the community centre.

Back George Street, Elswick, Newcastle, 1935. This photograph was taken for the slum clearance programme of the 1930s.

Poverty and Enterprise

'On February 10th 1911, I was born into the world of hardship and poverty.' Mrs D. Averill begins her story with these words, and they begin many people's stories. Mr Neilson, a Public Health Inspector, started work in 1934 and described some of the public health issues he found regularly in Gateshead:

> When I first started I went in at the tail end of a smallpox epidemic. But as that died out we got another problem and that was diphtheria. Then again, the transfer of these diseases was largely due to the way people were living in close packed houses and their general state of health was lowered because of these conditions and they were infecting each other quite quickly.

He was involved in inspecting the slum dwellings and moving families to better conditions:

> I remember being in this particular house down Hillgate and there were some old pictures on the wall. For some reason I just pulled a picture off the wall and behind it was a brown mass of bed bugs, just a brown mass, that just fell down. They were there during the day and came out at night. And all the pictures would be the same.

Hooky and proggy mats were the product of poverty, of having little but needing a lot. Yet, like many contributors to this book, Mrs Averill's memories are not bitter or unhappy ones. She was the second child of a large family and because she was a girl:

> I had more or less to take on the responsibility of the younger ones. But apart from that I have wonderful memories of my childhood. Dad worked in the shipyards and money was scarce, so Mam started making hooky and clippy mats then raffled them for money to keep us. She also helped make them for the Church funds. All of us had a portion of the mat to work before we could go out to play. I was married in 1947 and she made me a large one for a wedding present. Now at the age of 93, I often sit and think of those bygone days.

Mats, whether plaited, knotted, hooked or progged, appear to have developed independently around the poorer areas of most European countries. Different styles of matting can be seen in many parts of Europe and America from the middle of the nineteenth century onwards. In Britain, wages in agriculture and mining were low and bought carpets were expensive, so mats were seen in every working-class home. They were ideal covering for the cold stone floors of pit cottages and farmhouses.

Life was hard whether urban or rural, so although people were aware they were poor, it was relative because everyone was poor. One benefit for the miners was free coal; often the fire was both heat and light for some families:

Raking through rags at Ouseburn tip, Newcastle, 1907. Despite the obvious poverty the little boy is wearing a smart celluloid collar, cap and boots.

The memories were of my dad's mother sitting in her cottage at Westwood, making her clippy mats on a frame in front of a large coal fire. She would always work this way because her husband, being an ex-coal miner, got his allocation of coal free. She would never use the electric lights in the cottage if it could be avoided. When the electricity company called to read the meter it was little more than a shilling for four months. *Memory Book*

Running out of money for the electric or gas meter was a common problem.

When the pennies ran out, the light from the gas would suddenly go out. *Memory Book*

Candle light was a common substitute, or simply managing by the light of the fire. Whole families would go to bed early on a Thursday night (before payday Friday) because they didn't have a penny to put in the meter. Heating water in the boiler to fill the tin bath was a longwinded process too and sharing bath water was usual for children.

It was a nightmare getting baths – especially on Friday when everyone wanted to be out. My brother, who had a girlfriend, wanted to be first. *Memory Book*

Every domestic job was hard work. On washday the women did the washing in a big boiler, which first had to be lit underneath. The whites were washed first, then they stayed on a bench, while the coloured clothes were washed, and when everything was finished and the water emptied out, the boiler was filled with cold water. The 'Dolly blue' bag was dabbled in the clean water, then the whites left in that all night so the frost would make them whiter still. They were starched the next day.

The clothes would be hung on lines stretched along the back lane, and as most women did their washing on the same day, a whole lane would be filled with drying sheets and clothes:

> If the coal man came to deliver coals that day there were ructions. If it was raining, a great big fire would be on in the kitchen and all the washing strung up there. Coming home at lunch time from school, the oil base would be on the table and you had to dodge in and out of the washing. Friday was bottoming day; the stove was black leaded, all the brasses polished, the door step was whitened and woe betide anyone who dared step on it. *Memory Book*

Young women and girls found work in service, doing the domestic work for the better off:

> I was fourteen. I left school in the December and the beginning of January I had a job. This was on Low Fell, and I did all the housework; washing, ironing, cooking. And I got four shillings a week. *Lillian Johnson*

> We lived in back-to-back miners' cottages with only one bedroom for the whole family. No modern facilities, a poss tub for a washer and a tin bath to bathe in, a toilet in the backyard and water collected from the tap in the middle of the street. Our neighbours who lived out the back of us had their bedroom window in our yard and ours was in theirs, us kids had great fun climbing in and out of the windows into each other's homes. We lived with Grandma because Dad was away seafaring at the time. My Mam grew vegetables and kept hens. Charlie the cockerel used to come in the kitchen and lift up his wing to get warm at the fire. When Grandma was upstairs making the beds he hopped up the stairs, one at a time. Most of us grew up to be hard-working decent people, most leaving school and starting work at the age of fifteen. Not many went to university as poor mining

Washday, early 1900s, with poss tub and dollies.

These women and a dog are outside miners' cottages in Dunn Street, Coxlodge, Newcastle, 1950s.

families couldn't afford it but some did go to further education in the local technical college. I didn't have my own bedroom until I was almost twelve years old when the colliery houses were pulled down and we were all moved into newly built council houses with all mod cons. This, I think, was the start of the demise of the mining community as we knew it. *Memory Book*

People were used to hard living and would think nothing of long walks to school at a very young age:

I was brought up in Cumberland, up in the mountains. I used to walk five miles to school when I was five years old. When it was dark or foggy my mother used to send the sheepdog down for me to make sure I got back ... The sheepdogs were bred to kill wolves, protecting the flock. A dog would be able to find a sheep trapped under a few feet of snow.

In most parts of the North East, heavy industry was the main source of employment. It provided work for men, and sometimes women, which was not only hard but frequently dangerous. If a man was injured in an accident, it could mean months off work or might even spell the end of his earning power.

I grew up in Washington – there were three pits, a chemical works and steel works. My father was a miner, then had an injury and went to the chemical works. Any miner who got injured was put up on a stretcher with wheels and pushed through the streets (covered with a blanket) until they were brought to their own house. Not many people went to hospital then. *Memory Book*

An accident for the man of the house meant the woman had to become the breadwinner. A woman would turn her housewifely skills to use – more often than not this was domestic work, cleaning houses,

This beautiful tiger was made in Cumbria, probably in the 1970s.

taking in washing, and making mats to sell. Many women would have two or three jobs and still have to look after the family:

> My father was in ill health, so my mam worked in the Walker Naval Yard to provide for us – she was a welder's tacker. She also worked as a domestic in the hospital in Walkergate, and at another time in Welch's toffee factory. On pay-day (Fridays) she brought a big bag of toffee misshapes home, and passed them among us – there were eight of us children. We lived in a two-bedroom flat. Our bath was in the scullery, with a top on to use as a work top. There were so many of us we had to take turns in the bath – three in the bath together and one in the boiler. *Memory Book*

There were many other ways families could create income, especially if they had a bit of land for an allotment or animals:

> My father also kept chickens. We used to buy the day-old chickens from the markets. There's certain hens called 'clockers' that would bring the baby chickens up. We used to brood the eggs under the hen, and in the middle of the night, fox it by taking two eggs out and putting two chickens in and the hen would bring them chickens up as though they were her own ... I used to love doing that bit, putting the chickens under the hen and she wouldn't know anything different in the morning.

> Another form of making money was to buy two dozen of these day-old chicks and bring them up and my father used to sell them. We used to try and buy the chickens round the February or March time but to keep them alive at that time me father had this ingenious device. He put tomato boxes on either side of the hearth and he had half a dozen feather mops suspended two or three inches off the floor so the chickens used to go inside the feather mops and be indoors. As the weather got better, we'd transfer them to the hen and let the hen bring them up; once they got to three or four weeks old they were strong enough to go straight to the hen. We used to sell them: people put their order in to us for

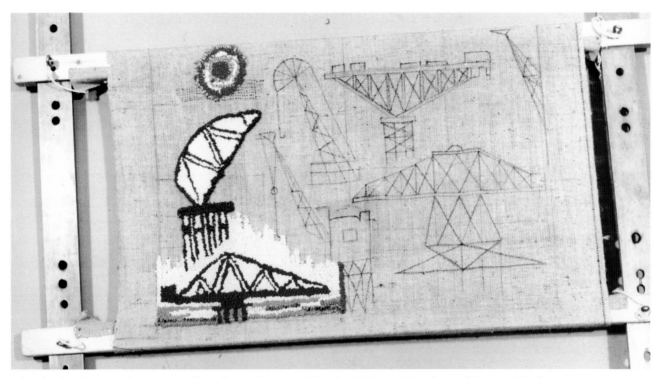

The shipbuilding tradition in Wallsend was illustrated by the Wallsend Hooky and Proggy Circle.

the hen for their Christmas dinner. Every hen was sold, every hen belonged to somebody in the street. We used to sell the eggs as well because me father was off work ill and there wasn't a lot of money. When my mother used to do all these jobs we also had the chickens to fall back on so we were never short of something to eat. *Bill Scope*

Britain in the 1930s was suffering from the world-wide depression, and areas of heavy industry, such as Jarrow, were hit hardest. Those out of work had to rely on the dreaded Means Test, a very strictly enforced method of deciding who would receive financial help from the Government. During these years, unemployment benefit lasted for twenty-six weeks; when this time was up, people were given transitional payments, subject to the resented Household Means Test introduced in 1931. The Unemployment Assistance Board was created in 1934, and was responsible for the long-term unemployed. The relief given, however, was totally inadequate and grudgingly given.

The wages of all family members, and any household assets, were taken into account when deciding whether or not relief should be paid. This meant that in some cases redundant men were dependant on their daughters or wives, a situation that did not fit in with the opinions of the time.

My father was on the Means Test at one time – during that time he made a boat for a timber merchant on the Tyne. He came from Finland, so his people knew about boat-building. My father used to go out between the piers at South Shields with a friend, some Sundays. I used to put on a miserable face, sitting on the fender, so that they'd let me go. 'Oh, go on then' my Dad said at last, and we took some sandwiches. While my Dad was on the dole, my mother made loads of bread and scones to sell – the Welfare found out and cut some of my Dad's dole. *Memory Book*

Every woman had to be thrifty in these hard times:

My father worked hard and earned two pounds fifteen shillings per week, half of which (not nearly enough) he gave to my mother to pay the rent and all living expenses. The other half went unfailingly into the pockets of the bookmakers who plied their trade at Brough Park Greyhound Stadium. *Memory Book*

There was a clear class divide in the mat maker's world:

If you were better off you would have a hand-woven Turkish carpet imported from wherever they came from. You can't imagine the Duke and Duchess of Northumberland sitting around doing proggy matting can you? No – but in the kitchen they wouldn't of been bothered about the servants – in the kitchen, the servants might … [have] made a proggy mat just so they had something on their feet you know. *Jo Wilson*

Help came from all sorts of places. Jo Wilson remembers the support that neighbours gave to each other in times of hardship:

My mother's father died when my mother was only ten so her mother had to go round scrubbing to make ends meet, and my mother had to look after the younger children, so they didn't make the mats themselves they were given them by the neighbours as presents. Very generous actually.

We always had dogs and there would be chickens walking along the top of the yard wall. My dad's pigeons were in Granny Corner's yard, in Vine Street. I remember Vine Mission, run by a woman, Sister Winifred, who did all kinds of great things for the people of Gateshead. *Bob Corner*

Selling mats, swapping labour

If the man of the house was injured or died in war, the woman would have to turn her hand to whatever she could; making mats would be a task she could combine with her family duties.

Ray Ditchburn remembers helping his Grandmother:

Well, I learned all about hooky mats, clippie mats, call them what you will, from me grandmother. She lived in Walker Street in Gateshead and they used to make mats for the family. But after me grandfather was killed in the First World War; she had to make mats to generate some income. And she would walk a couple of miles, with three six-foot mats, across to Newcastle and sell them in the Bigg Market. With the money she got from the mats she was able to pay for the penny tram back to Gateshead, and put some extra food on the table. So my granny taught me how to make a hooky mat, a clippie mat. She had four children to my grandfather; a babe in arms (my uncle Bill) and two other uncles and my mother. So she had to do something to get extra 'cos the money just wasn't there. If she had the cuttings, she'd knock up a mat in three or four days because she wasn't working alone. Because none of the family took sugar in their tea, and sugar was on ration, she had extra sugar which she used to make into cinder toffee and sweets. And the kids would come along, young teenagers, and help with the clippie mats and get a portion of toffee. So she was able, by using a bit of her ingenuity, to get stuff done. But that's how they did things then.

The Bigg Market, 1933.

Not only did Ray Ditchburn's grandfather die in the First World War, his father was injured in the Second:

> My mother used to make clippie mats because my dad had been in the Second World War and he'd been injured, so the couldn't go back down the pit. He had to take labouring jobs when he could get them. My mother had to make clippie mats for us to use and others to sell on.

Mat making was time consuming and laborious work. To turn out the number needed to make any money, women needed to enlist the help of others:

> I want to tell you about my granny, she was a 'tinker' – a very strict, severe woman. I'll tell you about how she got her clippy mats made. She would buy five Woodbines in a paper packet and would set up the mat frame in the wash house and place the cigarettes on the hessian. Well if you did some of the mat, you could have a cigarette. This was the 30's, the depression and times were hard; men were out of work and would do a lot for a Woodbine! She'd get a lot of work done for five Woodbines! This was in Jarrow and my father and uncle were on the Jarrow March – we're quite proud of them. *Memory Book*

Many mat makers relied on the help of children or family to get the mats finished to order:

> I remember my mother sitting every evening with the clippie mat frames, spread over two or three chairs. Either she was cutting up old clothes to make the mats, or hooking the pieces into the hessian. It was quite hard work, and I've seen her fingers bleeding from using the scissors. The mats were mainly for sale – a lot of them were sold through a local shop called Beavans. Also she used to make mats for our home. We all got involved with drawing the patterns. *Walter Wilkinson*

Mats for sale would use the better quality materials:

> I remember my grandmother making such mats, staying up all night to finish them to order. She used to make some of them from old chenille curtains and if you owned one of these you were very posh. *Memory Book*

> It was like finding the crown jewels if you found a black coat for the border. I remember she once made a stair carpet for a very rich lady. It was pink chenille with green borders – very chic fifty years ago. You knew it was Christmas soon when a new clippie mat appeared in front of the fire as the ones she made through the year had to be sold. *D. Sebastinelli*

Some mat makers were very protective of their mat – it had to be of a high standard if it was for sale:

> My mum was known in Murton as Hilda Honor and dad was known as Little Jackie Forster. He was father to four sons and four daughters but we were not allowed to help in any way when he and mum were making a proggy mat – it had to be just so. You see they earned seven shillings and sixpence for a three-yard

by two-yard size and that money was really needed to help feed us as dad was the only worker in those days. He was a miner and the only time he ever lost any work was when he broke his leg. Mind, we had the job of delivering the finished mats in the pram to the new owners. *Louie Farm*

However, the price they fetched didn't always reflect the amount of work that had gone into them:

The mat my Auntie made was six feet by four feet and all she got was thirty bob which is nothing today. *Memory Book*

Even when mat makers were offered money, sometimes the family needed the mat more:

Having made mats for years, I decided on a mat with a fruit design using part chenille and part clippings. On completion I was offered £80 which in those days (1954 or 1955) was a small fortune, but alas it had to

Wallsend Hooky and Proggy Circle demonstrating in Howdon in 1977. The lady on the left was one of sixteen. The mothers of both these ladies made mats to supplement the family income when they were children.

go on the floor – we were waiting for it. It was oblong with a half-moon within it. In those days, it had to be put on Father's bed, before it was put on the floor for Christmas. I was living in Washington; the only amenity we had was a wireless – no electric or gas, so we used paraffin lamps and candles. The toilet was forty yards down at the bottom of the garden.
Memory Book

Poor houses at Lemington, a village west of Newcastle, around 1900.

Enterprising mat makers would not only sell the finished product, but also make a little money out of providing the basics for others to make a mat. Some woman in the neighbourhood would make a business out of collecting clippings so she could sell them – she'd have them all sorted by colours in sacks with the top rolled down – and she weighed out what anyone wanted on some scales. Children would be sent there with a little scrap of material to get clippings that matched.

> In another street, a lady used to sell clippings. New material – I think it was remnants from clothing factories. It was sold by the pound or stone. When the sacks were empty they were sold. Her customers bought them for their mat backing. They would draw their pattern on then start filling in with clippings.
> *Memory Book*

Many stories show how desperate times were in the North East in the 1930s and 40s:

> This was not a hobby but a necessity as times were hard. In the forties my dad worked at Woodhorn Colliery but he had an accident that damaged his back and he was off work for months. Mam became our breadwinner until Dad was able to take on light work on bank at the Colliery. So Mam's mats were taken to the local sale rooms for auction. Today we take for granted the help and benefits we receive.
> *Memory Book*

Because the craft was associated with need and poverty, many found it hard to believe that others would pay for a mat:

> I can remember friends had a farm at Allendale. Violet's husband died and their son got the farm so she went to live in a cottage two fields away. Oh, beautiful, it was, a lovely house. But Violet didn't know how to fill her time in. She decided to make a mat, and so she looked – you see, in those days the material was so good, the tweed and that, there was no nylon or anything … she cut up a skirt and washed it. She finished this mat and her husband's cousin, who was the auctioneer in Allendale, said 'Violet, I'll sell your mat.' 'Oh no!' she says 'you cannot sell a mat.' He says 'I'll sell it for you.' She got seven-and-six for it and orders for another three. And I can always remember that's how Violet filled her time in. She used to go to a jumble sale or anything and unpick tweeds. *Edna Newman*

In some cases, the women had to hide their mat making enterprise from their proud husbands:

> I loved going to the jumble sales and I can still recall my mother's voice asking me to find nice bright colours. I used to get so excited and run to her when I found something really bright. She'd tell me I was a good lass with an eye for colour and she'd shush me off to find some more. We'd always buy more than we could carry and struggle back home laden. My mother's creativity meant there was always a proggy mat in the making. Her colourful designs were admired by many a neighbour and a request for a mat for a small exchange of cash would never be refused. The revenue it brought in was always welcome, particularly in the 1930s. My father had no idea my mother sold the odd proggy mat. He thought of himself as the breadwinner. He was a proud and gentle man but as far as the money was concerned he was a little frugal and knew nothing of my mother's cottage industry. Times were hard; money was scarce so the additional funds were most welcome; helping to keep those hungry wolves away from the door.
> *Margaret Kavanagh*

TWAM, Shipley Art Gallery

Working a proggy mat.

Lillian Johnson remembers seeing mats in the pawnshops:

> Cos I used to see the pawnshop down Gateshead. Not that me mother ever went in but I used to see these mats hanging in the pawnshop.

This reflects both how little people had to pawn, but also how highly the mats could be valued. If someone was known to be particularly skilled, they would get orders for rugs from the wealthier members of the community

> Say the doctor in the village needed a rug for his wife as a surprise for Christmas, he would come to see my aunt and order one. She wasn't allowed to say who she was making it for – it would be put away for Christmas first. *Memory Book*

Bartering and exchange were also a common way for poorer families to get what they needed:

> If someone in the back lane was handy and made a rocky horse for the family, she would make a clippy mat for his wife. *Memory Book*

Many necessary items were beyond the average income, and were bought with weekly payments, as they still are today from catalogues. In 1938 a new school uniform was an expensive item:

> My best friend (also called Joyce!) at Junior School won a scholarship to Morpeth High School. The joy of winning was marred by the fact that she had to have a school uniform. They simply did not have the five pounds that was needed. Mr Jacobsen used to call at their house. He would provide household items and clothing which was paid for in regular weekly payments. He had been calling there for a few years and was always given a cup of tea before going off to visit his other customers. When he heard about their problem he offered to loan them the five pounds and asked for five hooky mats in payment. Aunt Florrie agreed and she worked long hours, helped by neighbours and friends who would often call in and sit down at the mat and work along with her. Joyce got her uniform and took up her scholarship. Aunt Florrie cancelled her debt and Mr Jacobsen got his five large hooky mats. *Joyce Morgan*

However, as times grew more prosperous and financial circumstances improved, people's attitudes to the proggy mat changed. To capitalise on the skills of rug making, it was rebranded as a craft or hobby,

> I belonged to St. Silas Church Club as a boy; there were many activities, of which mat-making was one. *Memory Book*.

There were attempts to give it a more upmarket image. The advertisement on the page opposite, from the fifties, shows model Pi Leonard posing with a catalogue for Readicut rugs, from whom it was possible to buy a complete kit to make a fireside rug. In the postwar era, these rug kits were a step up from the old hooky mat. They came with a pattern book, they didn't involve a frame, but customers

Pi Leonard modelling for the Readicut Book of Rugs, 1951.

were provided with a stiff canvas and cut pieces of wool, a modern latch hook and a 'paint by numbers' stencil on the canvas. They were very expensive, so dispensing with the old 'poverty' associations. Despite the smart, modern appearance, it is easy to see the designs are not very different to those described by the contributors to this book, yet with less charm and originality. The advertisement demonstrates the attempts to turn rug making into a middle-class pastime for the better-off housewife, with leisure time on her hands. It couldn't be further from the 'rag mat as necessity' image that began this chapter.

However, for the older generation, the memories of hardship were too close. Mr Neilson, the Public Health Inspector testified to this:

> You often hear people say today 'it's worse than the thirties', well those people have no idea what the thirties were like, none whatever and I don't care who they are.

So for many people, rag rugs reminded them of really poor times:

> A lady I was talking to, she was about 93 said, 'Oh I don't want one of them in my house, it reminds me of when I didn't have any shoes on my feet and I couldn't go to school.' Yet her daughter absolutely loved them, she thought they were fabulous, because she didn't live in them times so she had no recollection of being that poor. *Margaret Atkinson*

A more recent story confirms this view is still prevalent.

> I was demonstrating my rug making on a stretcher frame one day at a show in Sunderland. Many people were coming and having a go, wanting to see if they still remembered how it was done. So many lovely memories were shared, mostly happy I am pleased to say. Later in the day, a lady was walking past my stand when she backtracked and stood looking at my rug in the frame. She said in quite a savage tone. 'I never want to see another of those as long as I live! We never got any tea the day my mother set a mat in the frame' then she stomped off. I had to laugh, but for her it was not a happy memory. Perhaps it reminded her of poverty and hardship. *Heather Ritchie*

'Ha'd on to your linings!'

'Your mother's making a mat!' Getting just the right colour, or enough of the material to finish a mat, was a constant issue for makers; it could drive an ordinary housewife to extremes, and the stories of coats and clothing being cut up by mistake are numerous. If someone's clothes were looking past their sell-by date, they might be told: 'It's about time that got ready to be put in the clippy mat.' Or when friends visited, they'd be teased: 'You can take your coat off you know, I'm not making a clippy mat.'

> Many times I heard the cry 'ye can tack yer coat off cos were not mackin' a mat,' This was always said to someone who didn't take their coat off when they came into the home. *Memory Book*

Irene Orton laughed when she remembered her mother kept a keen an eye on her friends' and neighbours' outfits:

> I tell you this is something she used to say. 'Oh, there's Mrs So-and-So, oh she's got a lovely red coat on. Oh, I'll have to ask her if she'll keep that for me, for me mat.' 'Scarlet,' she said, 'just the colour.' She used to look at what people were wearing.

Lillian Johnson remembers her mother saying to her brothers:

> Because they wore those linings you know, long johns. She would say 'ha'd on to your linings, your mother's making a mat'.

When the mat making season was in full swing, and a mat was planned, the hunt was on for the required colours in the right amount.

Ready-made clippings were in great demand everywhere, and when fresh bales of clippings were delivered to Shimelds in Stanley, Lorna and Ken Richardson remember customers would arrive in hordes. On one occasion, two ladies fighting over the same piece of material caused the department manager to take a pair of carpet scissors and cut it in half, thus settling the dispute.

Beamish Museum

The Proggy Mat

Beamish Museum

In days of old when nights were
cold, around the fire we'd sit.
Some women did embroidery and
others they would knit.
Some made a thing of beauty great,
as by the fire they sat.
And from a pile of clippings came,
the famous Proggy Mat.

Old jumpers, socks, and trousers
too, no, not a thing was bought.
God help the men who fell asleep if
she was clipping short.
She'd prog and prog with fingers
sore to get her mat complete.
'Hey Bella, where's my other sock? Ye knaa ah hev two feet.'

Now she'd be short of a bit of red, to finish off a Rose.
Jack's tie would be six inches short, just how nobody knows.
Bella's man turned out one night, in suit so smart and black.
A little patch of Emerald Green just showing at the back.

These makers of the Proggy Mats held nothing in respect.
To have it done by Christmas Day, no matter who they wrecked.
In Mauves and Greens and Blues and Reds, these Proggy Mats were made.
If she ran short of clippings, then it meant another raid.

You daren't go to bed at night when mats were on the go.
Ye dream't of Long John's with no legs, just walking to and fro.
As you lay there in sweet repose, sedated with Brown Ale,
The phantom progger struck again, along the clippy trail.

No fitted carpet looks this nice, the colours look a treat.
Don't you dare come another step, until you wipe your feet.
Pull up a chair, make yourself at home, don't sit on the cat.
Take off your shoes and curl your toes in your Mother's Proggy Mat.

If women ran out of colours for their mats, they would ask each other for a bit or swap material with neighbours. At the end of an evening, when the social gathering was over, people checked their belongings before they left:

> If we ever had visitors or relatives for tea, their coats were always laid carefully in the sitting room, over the best couch. On their departure they would always ask 'Where's my coat?' and up would go the cry, 'Me mother's put it in the mat!' *Memory Book.*

Nevertheless, recognising pieces of material in a mat was part of the pleasure. Children liked to try and identify and show everybody the bits that had been their clothes. This was a frequent joke among mat making families and neighbours, and, as the stories show, it wasn't always simply humour:

> Years ago when I was a girl and we lived in East Chevington in the colliery houses, my Mam made mats. One time she was missing a bit of grey, like the stuff trousers were made of. My Dad had come in from work and fell asleep in front of the fire, with his feet up on the stool. Mam cut off the bottom half of one of his trousers legs, to get on with finishing the mat. When he woke up he just couldn't believe his eyes and said 'Where's my other leg?' We have always laughed about it. *Olive Longhurst*

During the Second World War, many young men and women swapped their civilian outfits for uniforms, and went off around the country:

> I joined the land army, and was sent down South. Dressed in my uniform, I arrived at this farm house where I billeted with a number of other girls. They had their civvy clothes with them, to use when they went out for evenings. I sent a letter to my mother asking her to send my civvies down to me. They never arrived, so I went back home to collect them. When I asked my mother for my clothes she said she

Land girls, Stocksfield, Northumberland.

did not know where they were. I looked everywhere for them to no avail. Then I noticed a new hooky mat in the room. I also noticed it had been made with the aid of my civvy clothes. My mother redeemed herself by rigging me out with new civvies. *Olive Longhurst*

The need to finish the mat was placed above all other considerations, and many women felt no compunction about lying:

Dad was a hoarder – the cupboards were full of greyhound racing programmes, second-hand wood, screws, nails, rope, etc. etc. and his side of the wardrobe was crammed with the clothing of many years, most of which never saw the light of day. His navy blue suits were standard wear; the very old one for work and the not quite so old one for going to 'the dogs'. On a warm summer evening, Dad emerged from the bedroom after much banging of doors and enquired of my mother, 'Lizzie, I have a pair of light grey flannels somewhere but I can't find them'. Mother responded, somewhat unconvincingly, to the effect that it had been a long time since he had worn them, perhaps he had tried them on, found them to be too small and thrown them out. She would not have dared to suggest that he looked down and examine the new clippy mat on which he was standing! *Memory Book*

There were stories of mats being stolen off lines and walls … and long johns too!

We lived at Seaton Hirst, Ashington and in the olden days they used to hang the washing out in the back lane. One day there was a man selling Old Moore's Almanac and after he had been my father's long-johns were missing off the line – they would be wet mind. The police were called and they found the man beside the White Elephant pub and they took him into the men's toilets and retrieved the long johns. *Mary Sanders*

Jesmond Vale, 1937.

John Hipkin

In big families, clothes were handed down from sibling to sibling and were thoroughly used by the time they were cut up for mat clippings. It was rare for the youngest child to be bought anything new. Clothes were worked to the maximum.

> All my friends, the lucky ones where there was one child in a family, would get something new but I can very rarely remember anything I got bought new. With two older brothers, everything they used, I could use. The only time I can ever remember getting bought anything new was I was about twelve or thirteen and I got laid out with all new gear because I was to be going in hospital for an operation to take my tonsils out. The waiting list was years long then. I was eighteen or nineteen when I was sent for the tonsils, so the new clothes I got ended up too short when I came to use them. *Bill Scope*

That last little bit

Trevor Read and his sister remembered their mother's terrible search for the last bit of material to finish the mat:

> We both said we could remember her searchin' the house if she had a tiny bit left and she didn't have the right colour and she'd be through the drawers lookin' for a bit just to finish this mat off. *Trevor Read*

> A neighbour would come and say 'Mrs Anson have you got a little bit of black just to finish me mat,' and they used to lend each other – well give each other – a piece of black or a piece of red or whatever they wanted. *Lillian Johnson*

Ali Rhind

Making a proggy mat at Wallsend Community Arts Centre, late 1970s.

The habit of hanging on to material 'just in case' was strong and when Elizabeth Wilkinson was clearing out her mother's house after she'd died they found:

Sort of strips that were rolled up in brown paper and folded, tied with string – when she'd finished making the mats, she kept some pieces that would have gone on to another mat had she lived.

A typical miner's cottage, Charlotte Pit, Benwell, 1900.

Newcastle, March 1939. A family inspects its newly installed Anderson Shelter. Steel walls were sunk three feet into the ground and covered with the excavated earth. Although subject to flooding the Anderson would protect against all but a direct hit.

The progger on the opposite page was made from a bullet ... a case of swords into ploughshares?

World War Two Memories

The Second World War reshaped the economic and geographical landscape of Britain and touched everyone's lives. Most of the memories in the book come from people who were born either during or just after the war, so for many contributors to this book, the making of mats and wartime stories are intertwined.

> I was born under the stairs in a small miner's cottage at Edward Row, Hamsterley Colliery, Co Durham in October 1941 during World War Two. Bombs were falling nearby at Ebchester. I was apparently born in the same house as my father. *Memory Book*

Under the stairs was a common place to sit out an air raid, and often young children had to share the space with the mats, clippings and frames:

> My mam used to put us to sleep under the stairs during the war. She had a special mat in there and in the winter she would put one over us. A house got bombed near us. They were after the pit of course. In all the pictures of bombed buildings the stairs were always left standing, so my mam just reckoned it was safer for us to be under the stairs to sleep, all cosy on the mat. *Memory Book*

> During World War Two, when I was four years old, we used to help our mother with her proggy mats, cut clippings, put them in a bag under the stairs. When the sirens went off, we had to get up, go downstairs and we used to go under the stairs, and I always slept in the bag of clippings till the all clear. *Memory Book*

Of course, the very sources of employment – the heavy industries that kept the North East going – were targets for the German bombs: the pits, steelworks, rail yards and depots. It's not surprising that many remember the air raids:

> We lived in a small village (Pity Me). There was an ammunition dump at a smaller village (Brasside). In the mid-war years, German bombers tried to locate it. Some nights, during the blackout, when the mats were being made, the bombing started. The four children were bundled under the staircase, which was insulated with very hard cushions. One time they missed the ammo dump, and the bombs dropped adjacent to Earls House Hospital. The blast was so loud, we thought it was just outside. Mind you, half a mile away was very close. *Jim Winter*

For children, it often seemed an exciting time:

I didn't get evacuated because my mother didn't want me to go, but my two elder brothers were. My brothers were allowed to come home now and again for a visit. About 500 yards from where we lived was a defence field where they had lots of guns to protect the shipyards from the aeroplanes. Initially they just had the small guns and you could just hear the pom pom pom pom pom as the gun was going, but they mustn't have been effective for what they wanted – they dispensed with them and put the big massive guns in. When they first let them off, a lot of the houses lost their windows

An evacuation rehearsal on 29 August 1939, just before the outbreak of war. These Newcastle children are carrying their gas masks. On 1 and 2 September 44,000 children were evacuated to Cumberland, Northumberland and North Yorkshire; by 21 October 11,000 had returned to the city.

through the blast, so you ended up with big broad brown tape on all your windows to stop them cracking and the glass coming in. I remember when my brothers came home this particular weekend, after they had been away about a year, we were explaining to them how the guns went off and it would be frightening. I was teasing them, but they said 'No, I won't be frightened. I'm not frightened of guns'. Well, the first night they were home there was an air raid and we had to go into the shelters. Me and my mother and father were used to it, so we just got up and went to the shelters. One of my brothers came downstairs and fell off the bottom three stairs with no trousers on at all and the other one fell down the stairs with two legs in one trouser leg, he got such a fright. That memory is implanted in my mind for ever.

There was an amazing camaraderie with the shelters; my father was an ARP warden that patrolled the area to stop people letting lights show … and just at the bottom of the street from where we lived they had a big communal point where they met. They had cookers in it and they used to make broth, especially in the winter. So you would get a knock on your shelter door with your delivery of broth and they just kept cooking the broth and giving everybody a sup through the night.

Sometimes you used to go the shelter and, if there had been lots of rain, there would be water in the bottom and you couldn't always clean it out. They had bunks, and my father put a couple of extra bunks in so everybody was off the floor, and you weren't touching the water. To us it wasn't a war, at our age it was an adventure. *Bill Scope*

Alan Bays was born in 1939 and his early childhood memories were of war:

Once the air-raid siren started up, the whole family had to leave our blacked-out bottom flat to go into the

ARP Wardens practise for the anticipated fire and gas attacks, February 1939.

squat, brick-built air-raid shelter in the back yard. The family from the upstairs flat were there. What a musty smelling place it was, with hessian-draped bunk beds running along each side. I was glad to get out when the all clear sounded. Some buildings had been hit in the raid and all the talk at school the next day was about 'shrapnel,' which some kids had been able to find, though I never saw any of it myself. It's hard today to convey the mystique surrounding this commodity. If you were lucky enough to have found some then I suppose it would be equivalent today of being the only one in the class to possess the latest Harry Potter book! Little boy that I was, I didn't come out of the war unscathed. Over the entrance to the air-raid shelter hung an old quilt that my mother always told me to keep away from. I didn't. The quilt was held in place by a heavy brick on the roof and I pulled it down on myself. The corner of the brick hit me right between the eyes. Speechless, not so much with pain as with fear of what my Ma would do to me for disobeying her, I made for the door to the back lane quietly. But the strange silence following the sound of the brick hitting the ground must have alerted my Ma. She came out but I didn't get wrong. I still have the scar on my nose to this day!

Despite the air raids, the mat making went on and Mr Hutchinson's story illustrates the bravery and stoicism of the communities who made them:

During the war a fire bomb dropped in the front street in Elswick. My mother had just made a mat and the old fashioned sinks always had the floor in front wet, so the mat, newly finished, was wet. She ran out into the street and threw it on the bomb. There was big fizz and the bomb burst through the mat. Mrs Danskin came up to lend a hand. The ARP man came along wanting to do it properly, crawling on his side coming from a distance with a hose. Mrs Danskin said 'Oh, give us the b…y hose here and we'll do it properly.' So two women put out the bomb and my mother cursed Hitler for the rest of the war for the hole in her mat.

The radio not only kept the families entertained while they made mats, they were also the all-important source of news about the progress of the fighting:

I remember when we were kids we liked two programmes on the radio. One was Dick Barton Special Agent and the other was Johnny into Space. Most of the time we were playing outside in the street. If somebody shouted that one of our programmes was starting we all dived into the house and sat round a little radio. On the winter nights we made mats. All we had for entertainment was a radio, and that radio didn't operate electrically. It ran off a battery similar to what's in a car. You used to have two batteries. One would be in the radio and you had to take the other to a place that charged it up again … I didn't realise what the significance was when bulletins came out about the war. I remember my father would say 'be quiet' because he was listening to the bulletin. It didn't interest us but … the minute the bulletin was issued about the war there had to be silence in the house. *Bill Scope*

Mats continued to be made and babies continued to be born, and people clung to their traditions:

I can remember my Grandma saying, during the war, that one of her neighbours had had a baby that hadn't been churched, and at that time people used to be superstitious about having a baby into the house that hadn't been to church. After the air raid warning had gone off this young mum was on her own. Her husband was at war. And Grandma said, come on, come on in. She didn't want her sitting in her shelter on her own with her new baby. I think that was the first time she'd had a baby into her house that hadn't been to church. But I think after that she realised that it didn't really make any difference you know. *Elizabeth Wilkinson*

During the war, sailors would have time on their hands as they travelled the across the oceans, and so they improvised the wherewithal to make a mat. Sheelagh Ward's father was at sea:

I always used to admire a navy blue and grey runner mat that my father had made on a warship, on the way home. He told me he'd made it out of parachutes, half dyed navy and the other half left grey. It was a

A bomb crater and severely damaged house at The Oval, St Anthony's, Newcastle.

ncjMedia

ncjMedia

Members of Heaton Social Service knitting garments for servicemen, 16 November, 1939.

diamond pattern, a large one in the middle and small ones on the outside. It never wore out.

The war, and its legacy, continued to loom large over people's lives long after it had ended, and for many it was a way of measuring time and developments in the community:

> For me Proggy mats have a very 'then and now' aspect; before 1940 and after. I clearly remember my parents sitting at a large wooden frame beside our kitchen window in our Edwardian upper flat industriously progging away, and my father carefully showing me how it was done. *Memory Book*

As peace began to reassert itself and normal domestic life resumed, the rug making that had been commonplace before the war slowly began to decline. The new Labour Government of 1945 and the establishment of the Welfare State changed people's circumstances and attitudes.

This was just after the War, we lived in Gateshead – they seem like quieter days. In fact, only a few cars came into the street; I do remember the bread van. The coal was brought with a horse and cart, and the ice-cream man pedalled a bike with the ice-cream at the front ... I suppose he had ice around it somehow to keep it cold enough. *Memory Book*

Material conditions improved in the communities where mat making had been the norm:

I was born in Newcastle, lived in Benwell, until I got married. My mother was a cook and my dad was a motor driver for the Corporation. I went to the local school, obviously primary school, then I went to Pendower Secondary school and I left when I was just coming up to sixteen then I went to work at Northern Electric. It had just recently been nationalised and everyone was cock-a-hoop because they had just got nice big rises. It was a good time to join really, wasn't it? I worked there until I was 26, not very exciting but that's what I did. Then at 26 I had my first child. *Mavis Jopling*

Mavis Jopling made the point that during the war no-one was able to purchase much in the way of anything pretty or nice:

It was all utility furniture. You had to be getting married or something like that before you could get the coupons to get your house put together a little bit, so it was a case of make-do-and-mend literally all the time.

This created the belief in thrift and careful hoarding:

You didn't throw away. You saved paper and you saved bits of string and everything. It's a habit, it's very difficult to get out of. A friend of mine said 'we were clearing John's mam's house and she must have saved everything!' Unfortunately for my friend, she lived in a house with lots of cupboards. She said it took forever. She said there were little bits of string – her mother-in-law threw nothing away, she kept newspapers and she kept brown paper. Obviously she felt that she still had to save everything, even though the war had been over for many many years. *Mavis Jopling*

For many, mat making stopped with the war and a removal to a more modern house, but as one person remarked 'I do not know which of these events was the trigger.' *Memory Book*

Rachel Phillimore

This elaborate mat depicting the Last Supper was bought in an antique shop in Hexham. It was made by two Cumbrian sisters, probably during the 1960s, and is quite large, around 8ft by 5ft.

Mat Rituals and Ceremonies

Some mats were pure works of art and if a maker was particularly skilful and artistic they usually had a waiting list from family, friends and neighbours for one of their designs, especially if there was a wedding or some special celebration coming off. Any big family occasion might be marked with a mat, either as a present or for furnishing the floor at the social event.

> I had two brothers and a sister and every time mam was pregnant she made a new mat for the baby being born. Maybe that's why I don't remember the frames in use, as I was the youngest. *Memory Book*.

It goes without saying that every household had a new mat for Christmas:

> Then the great moment arrived when it was all finished. It was usually just before Christmas when it was actually laid on the floor. Your house looked really posh ready for Santa Claus coming; not that we actually got very much, maybe an apple, an orange and some knitted gloves or mitts. That was it, but we had a brand new clippie mat to sit on to open our presents and that was pure luxury. *Mrs Glover*

Like Christmas decorations and the giving of presents, laying a new mat was one of the seasonal traditions and everyone had their own rituals to mark the occasion:

> On a holiday time, like Christmas, she would decorate the house and make new mats. For the bedroom, it would have flowers and a lovely border. The living room mat would be larger and when it was made, my mam and two sisters would put me in the middle and shake me up and down. *Brenda Porter*

TWAM, Shipley Art Gallery

89

Many people remembered rolling on the mat as a ceremony:

> Oh yes, my mother made lovely mats, and when it was finished it was a bit of a ceremony because it had to be unpicked out of the frame. And then I had to roll on it, you know. 'Come on then; get a roll on the new mat.' That was a little ceremony. I wasn't in my teens then. I would say twelve, maybe thirteen. I wasn't sort of grown up because I wouldn't have been rolling on a mat I don't think. But I can see her now, sitting, and she would talk away all the time that she was progging. We didn't have telly then so it was an interest, wasn't it. *Irene Orton*

Children used to run, shouting: 'I'm firsty on the mat!' Then all the children would take turns to roll over on it, and some had a name for this ritual: 'hanseling' remembers P. Khandaroo from Bedlington. The new mat by the fireside was a talking point, and a pleasure – to walk or sit and play on, enjoying the warmth of the hearth. There were many games devised using the new mat.

> I used to visit my Great Aunt's house with my Great Uncle. Every week we played our game using coins and the big proggy mat in the middle of the floor. The mat was made up of different coloured diamonds. If your coin landed inside the diamond shape you scored points. If it landed on the edges of the diamond you lost. I used to love playing this game and always remember winning. Thirty-five years later I introduced my niece to this game on my more modern rug. She also enjoyed the game for quite a few years, and funnily enough she always won. *Memory Book*

This next story gives a slightly different slant to memories of rolling on the mat!

> When talking about what to name babies, my grandmother Catherine Lorimer or 'Kitty' as she was known, asserted that children should be named after the place they were conceived. So far, so good. I lived in Bluebell Dene at the time so she said I should call a girl Bluebell and a boy Dene, ha ha. But then she decided maybe that might not be such a good idea as that would mean her son should be named 'Clippy Mat!' *Memory Book*

Dadding and dusting

Cleaning was done every week, and a big effort was made at the end of the winter months – the spring clean. Edna Newman, like most of the contributors, confirms that there was always a mat in for the winter, 'it was sometimes finished for Christmas or in the cleaning you see – spring cleaning.' But they don't do that nowadays, she concluded; spring cleaning as a seasonal activity has died out. However, in the days of hooky mats it was different. Mats in the kitchen, by the fire, in front of the hearth, or the range got heavy use from dirty pit boots, muddy allotment wellingtons, or just regular everyday wear and tear, and would need regular cleaning.

One method was to take the mat outdoors and either hang it over a line and beat it, or beat it against a wall, and it often took two people to handle the rug. Lillian Johnson said she sometimes got a neighbour to help her. She'd take one end and the neighbour had the other, and they shook the mat to get the dirt out: 'They had to be shook every day.'

This was known as dadding the mat:

> That was the main thing in a morning, shaking the mats in the street. One at one end of the mat and one at t'other shaking them up there. There was the clippy mats and the hooky mats, then the cocoa mat come on the go. *Mrs Rutter, Beamish Oral History Collection*

The mats were thick and weighed a fair bit, so they weren't easy to carry about and clean. A mat made with cottons could usually be cleaned with soap and water:

> We laid them flat in the cement yard at the back, got a pail of hot soapy water with cloths and scrubbing brush, they got a good scrub then a rinse. We then went over them with a dry cloth, and they were thrown over the clothes line or back yard wall to dry. Then they were as good as new. *Memory Book*

The Electricity In Service Exhibition, Newcastle, 1924.

My grandmother's house was carpeted entirely with hooky mats. The patterns of the hookies were all the same, so that they were joined to one another to look like one big carpet. Made with plate patterns, the background was cream (the worn long johns). She wouldn't allow them to be swept with the Ewbank carpet sweeper, or shaken very often, but they were brushed with the hand carpet brush. Perhaps that's why they lasted more than a lifetime. (Memory Book)

More fun in the snow than cleaning the mats! Newcastle, 1920s.

Others washed them in the bath, or more recently, the washing machine.

Another method on wintry days would be to take the mat out on a frosty morning and drag it over the icy grass to clean it. Ali Rhind remembers a trip to Allendale on a very frosty morning and seeing mats laid out over the wall: they had been washed with soapy water, then left to freeze. When they were subsequently cracked, the muck came off with the ice. Most women had their methods, ever resourceful when they lacked the modern day appliances we take for granted.

> The beautiful patterned, multicoloured mat that was developing on the frame bore little resemblance to the dust trap, mangy looking thing that sat in front of our range. I can't remember seeing a vacuum cleaner in those days, not in our house anyway. *Memory Book*

These mats sat on the brown lino for years in our kitchen. Indestructible. They were taken outside regularly to clean. The big one (about 3 yds x 4 yds) was hung over the railings to air, and the smaller ones were bashed against the wall by my Mam wearing her wrap-over pinny and her turban to keep the dust and grime out of her hair and hide the metal curlers. *Memory Book*

Elaine Robson

Cleaning the mat was a regular job that could be entrusted to children:

She mended some of the regular holes burnt in by the hot sparks and coals from the fire, but towards the end of its life there would be 'more holes than rug.' Each week my next job was to take the rug up the garden, hang it over the washing line and beat it with the carpet beater. One day my mother came with me and must have been having a chat not suitable for my ears, when I came in with the beaten rug. 'That's not clean – you haven't been five minutes. Get out there again and do it right,' shouted my mother. I beat it so well it fell in half! My Granny laughed till her sides ached but my mother was furious. I got a good skelping when we reached home. *Memory Book*

Mats for special days

Because mats got such hard wear, they were often rotated about the house, to keep some in better condition for visitors:

My mother always had two for the fireside. You had your Sunday one, the weekend one, and then perhaps a less special one for weekdays. *Memory Book.*

Margaret Atkinson from St Mary's Proggers Group in Gateshead remembers something similar:

Sometimes when you made a proggy mat you turned it up one way during the week and then on Sunday you turned it up the other way because that was the posh side, but a hooky mat is the same on both sides.

Proggy mats were often given to mark special occasions, such as marriages, births and anniversaries. The Memory Book contained many little snippets like this:

We were given a proggy mat when we were married, specially made by my husband's grandmother. It was a black background with lovely coloured tulips worked in the corners.

My husband was an upholsterer; he worked all day and did odd jobs at night. It was 56 years ago he did a job for a lady who made clippy mats, and guess what I received as an engagement present – yes, a clippy mat that had pride of place in our bedroom by the side of the bed.

A finished mat became the focal point in front of the fire, a topic of conversation and admiration.

My mother completed a particularly beautiful mat one year, black borders and roses in the middle. She was so proud of it, it lay at the fireside for all to see. This was the winter of 1959, and as my older sister was always 'twisting' for a dog, she got her wish. A neighbour took her to the Cat and Dog Shelter and she brought home a cross-spaniel, Monty, who was to be a faithful companion for 16 years. However, his first night in our home ended in disaster. Ma got up as usual at 6.00 am, as women with a big family and a pitman husband used to. We got up early too. The screams were horrendous. We scattered down the stairs as fast as our little legs could carry us. Imagine the sight – dog cowering in the corner of the kitchen, all eyes and quaking – and there in the middle of a sea of chewed up clippings stood my mother. Her beloved mat was in tatters. From then on Monty was banned from the kitchen every night and had to sleep in the cupboard under the stairs with the door firmly shut and the offending mat thrown in for comfort! We often laughed about it. Monty thereafter could never settle anywhere else to sleep and always sat outside the cupboard when he was ready for bed. *Ann Cosker-Craig*

A hooky mat from both sides.

A bedside mat, for lighter wear.

Old Tales, New Beginnings

Wallsend Hooky and Proggy Circle

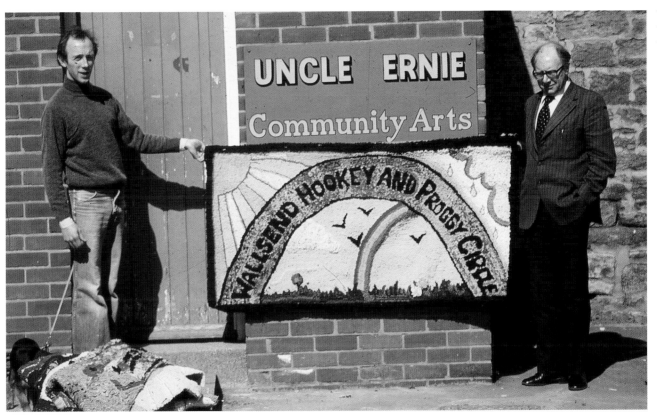

Ali Rhind

One day in 1977, while working as a community artist in Wallsend, I attended the local leek show, and saw a number of proggy mats there – I'd never encountered them before. I got talking to a lovely elderly gentleman who had won the prize for his mat. He invited me back to his house for tea and to show me his wife's mats (she had won the prize every year until this one, and had only recently died). While we chatted he opened a drawer to reveal the worn down horn proggers that represented all the mats that they had made side by side over the decades. Inspired, I went away and advertised for folk to join a mat making circle. Wallsend Hooky and Proggy Circle was born in Wallsend Art Centre in Charlotte Street, and met and made together over the next five years. *Ali Rhind*

Ali Rhind told the tale of a stag and a whippet from Wallsend Hooky and Proggy Circle.

Two members of the circle, Peggy and Ivy, wanted to make a mat based on a painting of a stag at bay so I drew them a design. The stag was lovingly made and duly finished, but by then Ivy was in hospital. So, to cheer her up, Peggy and I decided to take the mat to show Ivy. I carefully rolled it up and rested it on top of the car while I settled Peggy into her seat, and off we went. On arrival at the hospital – no mat! I had left it on top of the car and of course it had rolled off during the journey … I was devastated.

What to do? My flat mate had the idea of phoning local DJ James Whale on his late night radio show to ask for help and to request anyone finding the mat to phone me. Later, I got a phone call: 'I've got yer mat. If yer want it back come to the Black Horse pub at Windy Nook and we'll do a deal.'

So off I went to Windy Nook, and a deal was made, to make the Rising Sun Whippet Club a mat in exchange for the stag at bay mat, and yes, we made the whippet mat.

Top, the Stag at Bay on its hessian backing, and right, Ivy working on the mat for the Rising Sun Whippet Club.

Ali Rhind

Ali Rhind

Peggy Webber made a special portrait mat to celebrate her golden wedding anniversary. Peggy's husband, Walter, is shown in his blue boiler suit. When Peggy was fed up with him she would stamp her foot on Walter and feel much better!

The Wallsend Hooky and Proggy Circle grew very popular and several other circles started up all over North Tyneside.

... And other memories from the past

A Public Health inspector would get to see a lot of sights during his working life and this memory is from Mr Neilson who worked for Gateshead Council and was visiting the steep streets around St Cuthbert's village during the 1930s and 40s:

They were so steep that most of them had a handrail on the curb, it was an iron tubular handrail for people to pull themselves up the street with. Some of the streets were actually built in long steps, steps of about three feet wide and a step up. I remember going there and it was a winter's day, the roads were slippery and right down one side of the street, all of the tenants had brought out their clippy mats, you know the old clippy mats and they were laid on the pavement and it stopped about half way up the street. I wondered what it was for, and it turned out that there was a funeral in that house and when this happened and the streets were slippery, they put their mats out so that the people could bring the coffin out and carry it down the street, walking on the mats to stop them slipping. That was a regular practice in that steep street, probably lots of places did the same thing.

TWAM, Shipley Art Gallery

The steep streets of Gateshead around 1900. Note the mats hanging from the balcony.

Like the seasons, every activity had its allotted time and meaning, often focused around the workplace. The Durham Big Meeting or Gala is an annual July celebration, when all the pits march with their banners and brass bands through the city of Durham to hear their trade union leaders and other politicians speak:

> About 30 years ago we used to take the Kelloe banner into Durham for the Big Meeting. All along the way at other villages the banner was paraded, before the miners visited each Club for a pint, and then got on the bus for Durham – as many as would fit on a double-decker in a tight squeeze. In Durham the banners were paraded and stopped outside the County Hotel, where all the dignitaries were. All along the way the brass bands were playing till everyone was at the race course – for the rest of the day the men got palatic and women and children had picnics. *Ted Wilson*

> My father was a merchant seaman, and he was away a lot of the time obviously. He died four years ago, but all his working life was spent at sea in the Merchant Navy. So I have various things at home that he's brought back. A lot of them have been passed on, but I have a whale's tooth – they were once in the Arctic and they met up with a whaler. The Captain on the whaler said that he'd just caught a whale and he asked if there were any men on board with children. My father was the only one so they presented him with a whale's tooth, which I treasure. *Lynn Swift*

Rugs to rags

The life of an old mat went on and on:

> First it would go on the bed, on the bottom of the bed to keep you warm, then off the bed it would go on the floor, then from the floor it would got into the front room, then it would go into the kitchen and eventually it would end up out in the nettie, which is the toilet. It would take years; it would stay for a long, long time. *Anne Sedgewick*

When rugs were really worn out, they often found their way into the garden or allotment. A leek trench would be dug and the old mat left to rot at the bottom. This both fed the leek roots and helped retain water. Sometimes a 'special recipe' would be added, though these were often kept secret in the competitive world of vegetable growing and showing. Alan Simpson told us that gardeners used old mats for the cold frame. It was fixed under the lid (made from an old window) of the cold frame. Beside the frame there was a bucket of water with a piece of old sacking draped in it and extending up to the mat. The water would be absorbed up the sacking into the mat which would then drip into the earth beneath the young cucumber and courgette plants. In this way there was constant moisture, darkness and the best conditions for seedlings.

If mats were falling to bits and nobody wanted them, then as Lillian Johnson said:

> Well I suppose the rag men would take them away. The rag and bone men used to come round the doors and shout 'any chappy stone!' That's step stone. 'Any chappy stone!' 'Cos we used to wait for him saying it, and we used to say 'what do you feed your horse on?' and of course he used to say 'Chappy stone'. Just when we were kids.

A hooky mat inspired by the leek and pigeon clubs, by Ali Rhind.

I remember very well the rag man coming around with a horse and cart full of rags and the children would all run out with a jumper or something and in return for the jumper or coat they would get either a goldfish in a plastic bag or a balloon and the rag man would sell the rags to the lady that was making the clippy mats in the lane but, of course, as a child you didn't realise what was going on. Often we would find something, if mum was out we would just take something and take it out so we could have a balloon which was naughty, it wasn't what you were supposed to do, but often she would find out because a couple of weeks later she would see it in a rug somewhere. This often happened. I remember going out and seeing the rag man and always scouting around for something about because I wanted a balloon or fish but the fish would never live. You could find a big old bowl to put it in but a couple of days later it was gone because your mum had put it down the toilet because it was dead. You couldn't afford to keep yourselves really never mind a fish so it was hard times. *Norma Bell*

Rag and bone men, Ethel Street, Newcastle, around 1966.

As times changed, innovations arrived; some remembered the early sixties when mat patterns were applied with iron-on transfers. As times grew more prosperous the need for making rugs diminished.

> Grandmother stopped making rugs around the seventies. When she first moved into the house she had lino floors, and she could not afford carpet. Actually they had a couple of larger rugs that would have been mats. As people after the war started going back to work, the money started to come in, the prices of things actually fell, so she could afford to buy carpet throughout. Even now she has the proper carpet and she has rugs to protect it; she has had this carpet for twenty years and it is immaculate because the rugs get changed but the carpet is still pristine. *Memory Book*

After the war, with the increasing prosperity of the 1950s and 1960s new jobs became available, the old communities started to fragment as people moved up in the world, and moved house. Wages improved and were spent on fitted carpets – an important sign of wealth. Thus the proggy mat became synonymous with poverty.

> My dad did not work in the mines, he was an electrician. When we moved to Billingham, he obviously got more money because I remember getting carpet then and that was a huge thing, an absolutely huge thing. We had brought one of the proggie rugs from our old house and it went into one of the bedrooms, but in the living room we got a carpet. *Helen Webster*

Elizabeth Wilson regrets that:

> ... when mum moved in 1973 the frames were left in the house and what happened to them I do not know. Only the small bedroom mats went with them and survived as, by then, they had enough money to buy carpets.

Owners of mats found new uses for their hard-wearing floor coverings:

> We've still got a few of her mats in the bottom of our shed – to put down on the lawn when the grandbairns come to play. *Memory Book*

> She kept on making mats right till she died, at age 86. Some of her recipes are still in the family – 'Tatie Cake' is a firm favourite ... a toffee tin (shallow), pastry bottom and top with filling of THIN potato, onion, bacon, butter. *F.B. Bell*

Many people remembered the cupboard under the stairs where bags of clippings and the tools and frames were kept, and later on, when no longer in regular use, the attic where they were stored. Now, the tools and frames are hard to come by:

I'm now in my fifties but about twenty years ago an old neighbour of ours asked me did I want her mat frames as she was too old to be bothered. Imagine my delight! I stored them in our garage, just for the time being you understand, till I could find a fitting place for them when I got back home from work. Unfortunately when I came home I was dismayed to find the frames gone. My darling husband, Mac, on seeing the 'bits of owld wood thought they'd do for the fire, pet,' had chopped them up to pieces. *Ann Cosker-Craig*

Ali Rhind

A brand new frame in use at a beginners' course, 2010.

Old skills, new inspirations

And as the need for the mats has faded, so the function has changed:

> My youngest sister (who now lives in Canada) makes beautiful wall hangings using the skills my Mam taught us when we were girls.

The WI is still going strong in the twenty-first century and is part of a movement to keep the old skills alive, arranging workshops on mat making. Lynn Swift got interested this way:

> In Newton Aycliffe where I live, they were having taster sessions of various crafts at the local library, and one was rug-making with Heather Ritchie. So I went along one Friday morning for a couple of hours, met Heather, and was quite intrigued. I'm a member of the WI and I'm on the executive committee, and I mentioned it there, in fact at one of our craft committees. And we invited Heather to come along to the WI House in Spennymoor, and she spoke to a lot of people. Two friends were there, and Heather told us about the class at Clayport Library so we just joined up. We very much enjoy doing it, it's something very interesting, and a social thing as well.

Rachel, who recorded this next story from Cath Blundell, explained the significance of artist Winifred Nicholson to the history of rug making: 'She certainly brought the art back into another sphere.'

Cath Blundell is the daughter of Janet Warwick who used to work for Winifred Nicholson. Janet's father was a farmer and it was in his house that Winifred first saw mats being made as an everyday activity. Janet would make mats in the 1940s and 1950s to Winifred's designs. Cath remembers when a bull picture was being made on a mat, how her brother

Jo Nelson

A Winifred Nicholson design for a bull, made by Janet Warwick.

would comment on the accuracy of the shape (or not as the case may be!). As a child, Cath lived in Lancashire and she remembers they were the only family with a frame and her school friends would be intrigued. One of her favourite designs was of a tiger; a bright orange had to be found and she remembers her orange woollen skirt being cut up for it.

Norma Bell makes the same point about the resurgence of mat making as an art:

> When you think about age, clippy mats started as clippy mats and ended up as being clippy mat pictures for the wall. We are now making clippy mat handbags and clippy rosettes. We have laminate flooring and lots of people are buying old cottages and trying to restore the floor. Even on holiday in a cottage now, it is lovely to see a clippy mat, because we are bringing the past into the future and that's what we want to do now. Bring the past into the future so that generations can see.

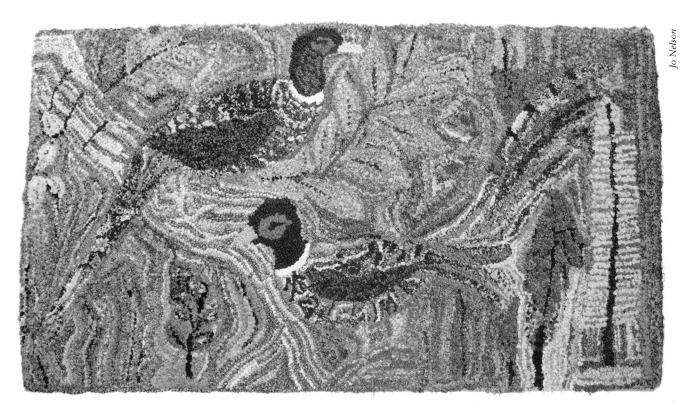

Jo Nelson

This beautiful pheasant was designed by artist Winifred Nicholson and made by Barbara Day.

Rachel Phillimore worked with the Bellingham Carers Group to make this sheep.

Though proggy or hooky mats are now rarely made out of necessity, or as a routine household task, as they were for countless generations of working people, that spirit of co-operative creativity, of intuitive pleasure in colour, texture and pattern, and making something beautiful out of very little, just refuses to disappear.

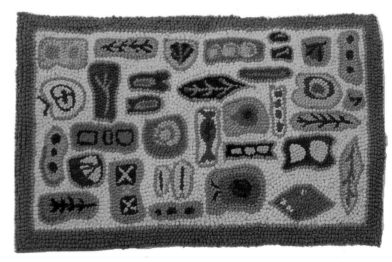

A Living Craft

That mat making, in all its forms, survives and flourishes in the twenty-first century is a testimony to the lasting attraction and the creative potential of the traditional craft. The resurgence of interest in mat making is partly about the recycling of materials – making something beautiful from worn-out clothes or remnants that may have had other lives as blankets or furnishings. There is also the impetus to work with wool, and to be creative with dyes.

Its also a wonderful vehicle for collaborative projects – the coming together is as important as the outcome.

Many new mat making groups have sprung up in the North East of England, and all around the country, in many different community settings from schools and hospitals to libraries and village halls.

Its potential as a contemporary art form is also being developed, not only in the form of mats, but as wall hangings, and soft furnishings.

Ali Rhind

A friendship mat created by John F. Kennedy School, Washington.

Ali Rhind

Working with seven-year-olds at Whitley Memorial School, Bedlington.

Above, 'Instance' a proggy wall hanging by
Rachel Phillimore.
Below left, reception seating for the Arts
Council North East by Ali Rhind.
Below right, two chairs made in
collaboration with Hepple Furniture by Ali
Rhind.

'Sustenance', a proggy wall hanging commissioned by the Community Foundation for the new Newcastle City Library, sponsored by Ryder Architecture. The wall hanging was taken round the region to Community Foundation events where over 400 people put clippings in.
Artists Ali Rhind and Rachel Phillimore.

Looking Back

The memories in this book have their origins all over North East England, and sometimes beyond, and span more than a century. Almost 200 handwritten and oral histories were collected over ten years as part of **Room For You Hospital Arts** at the Northern Centre for Cancer Care and the General Hospital, Newcastle upon Tyne, working with patients and their families and friends. Ellen Phethean was given the difficult task of choosing the extracts that most vividly illustrated the importance hand-made mats once played in people's lives.

Lucy Milton, who worked with the collections at the Shipley Art Gallery, Tyne and Wear Museums, in the 1970s, concluded her research into the history and craft of mat making with the words 'unfortunately such customs are now extinct' – but the craft *has* survived, transformed into art or enjoyed for pleasure, and practised by many groups in the region and elsewhere.

This celebration of mat making is not some nostalgic yearning for past years, but a record of individual remembering as well as the craft itself.

Silvie Fisch, Project Co-ordinator

This is a two-part wall hanging hung within the Northern Centre for Cancer Care at the Freeman Hospital. They were made with patients and their friends and families as part of the work with Room For You Hospital Arts based in the waiting area of the Radiotherapy Department.

The designs are based on medicinal plants that are used in cancer treatment.

The Contributors

Making a mat together, at Woodhorn.